Zabbix Performance Tuning

Tune and optimize Zabbix to maximize performance

Luciano Alves

PUBLISHING

BIRMINGHAM - MUMBAI

Zabbix Performance Tuning

Copyright © 2015 Packt Publishing

First published: June 2015

Production reference: 1250615

Published by Packt Publishing Ltd.
Livery Place
35 Livery Street
Birmingham B3 2PB, UK.

ISBN 978-1-78398-764-1

www.packtpub.com

Credits

Author
Luciano Alves

Reviewers
Gabriele Armao
Jean-Jacques Martrès
Renjie Yao

Acquisition Editor
Reshma Raman

Content Development Editor
Adrian Raposo

Technical Editors
Tanmayee Patil
Shiny Poojary

Copy Editor
Vikrant Phadke

Project Coordinator
Kinjal Bari

Proofreader
Safis Editing

Indexer
Rekha Nair

Graphics
Jason Monteiro

Production Coordinator
Melwyn D'sa

Cover Work
Melwyn D'sa

Foreword

Zabbix performance tuning is an important topic when it comes to the use of Zabbix to monitor a large number of network devices. I think most Zabbix users have experienced performance-related issues in some way or the other. These can be because of non-optimal configuration parameters of the Zabbix server or proxy, use of default settings for MySQL, the PostgreSQL configuration, or other reasons.

This book is quite unique. It focuses only on performance-related topics, and does so extremely well. Luciano is one of the most knowledgeable and active Zabbix users and community members. The first time I met him was in Brazil in 2008, and I was impressed by his deep understanding of Zabbix's internals and the great ideas that he always has. He has a unique combination of real-world experience and a strong technical background.

Regardless of how you use Zabbix and the size of your deployment, this book will give you enough information to be confident that Zabbix will deliver the level of scalability you need.

Read it; you won't be disappointed!

Alexei Vladishev
Creator of Zabbix

About the Author

Luciano Alves is Brazilian. He lives in the city of Porto Alegre in southern Brazil. He has been a Zabbix evangelist since 2007. Since 1994, he has been working to support the ICT infrastructure using his expertise in targeting and monitoring platforms. Luciano has had Zabbix professional certifications since 2008, and in 2012, he became one of the first official instructors outside of Zabbix SIA. He has trained over 200 professionals from different countries (Brazil, Argentina, Uruguay, Ecuador, Chile, Spain, and Colombia) to work with the Zabbix monitoring platform.

He is the founder of Unirede Soluções Corporativas, one of the main global partners of Zabbix SIA and currently the only premium partner in all of the Americas. Luciano is also a speaker at open source events, always talking about Zabbix. Besides this, he is a moderator of the official Zabbix forums in Portuguese and Spanish, and has worked on the translation of the official documentation into Portuguese.

Acknowledgements

No doubt, this book would not have been possible without the support of the competent technical body of Unirede Soluções Corporativas. These brave warriors were indispensable, discussing and supporting the testing and proof of concepts that were performed to support the content of several chapters. Then, there is also a special mention for Mr. Alisson Oliveira and Mr. Thiago Melo, who have always been willing and open, even without knowing the main objective of the proposed discussions and tests.

The list of thanks is actually huge, ranging from Leandro Santos, who gave me the opportunity to enter the world of ICT in 1994, to all the colleagues and bosses who came across me and helped me build the professional profile I have today. I also extend my thanks to Mr. Alexei Vladishev. In 2008, he boarded a plane in Latvia and disembarked in Brazil for the first official training in this region, and also believed in the goal of Unirede Soluções Corporativas — to become the world's best partner of Zabbix SIA. Then, thanks to Mr. Ricardo Santos (`http://zabbixzone.com`), who was initially invited to write this book but kindly passed on this challenge to me. I also wish to thank the active participants of the Zabbix Brazil community. They have served as the basis for a lot of information and statistical data given in this book. Not least to mention for writing this book are the competent professionals from Packt Publishing. They showed a lot of patience and supported and encouraged me, and I can only imagine how hard it must have been to deal with all the delays and disagreements that occurred during the process.

An honorable mention goes to our translator, Thiago Pitoni, for being part of this project, always suggesting new approaches, and rephrasing many sentences. Most importantly, thanks goes to my family, who were deprived of my attention and presence for a long period of time but never ceased to encourage and support me in this project.

About the Reviewers

Gabriele Armao works at Systematica, which is a Zabbix Premium Partner company that has always implemented system monitoring infrastructure. He chose Zabbix and developed many tools and scripts around it. He became a Zabbix-certified specialist on large environments in November 2010. In November 2012, he decided to move ahead and became a certified Zabbix trainer. For more information, visit the website at `http://www.gruppofinmatica.it/zabbix/`.

Jean-Jacques Martrès is an experienced IT professional who has a solid background (more than 10 years of experience in various ISP and carriers), both from a technology perspective as well as from a business perspective. For any architecture and technology, he can identify the needs and develop new high-value services. He is a self-made man and fast learner. Jean-Jacques specializes in building visions for what technology can make possible, how it will impact a company's business area, and how to obtain the maximum value from such changes.

Besides using and deploying Zabbix in different environments, he is also a maintainer of a great collection of templates. They are available at `https://github.com/jjmartres/Zabbix/`.

Renjie Yao lives in Shanghai and has worked for eBay (as an intern), PPTV, and Vipshop (since 2011). Vipshop (`http://www.vip.com/`; VIPS in NYSE) is one of the biggest e-commerce companies in China. It operates as an online discount retailer for various brands. Renjie is a full-stack engineer, who loves backend architecture and frontend visualization work.

At PPTV, he was in charge of Zabbix and he fixed bugs in the Zabbix kernel on Oracle. He worked on real-time calculations and architecture design on big data. Nowadays, his main focus is on machine learning, which is used to diagnose issues by machines, not human beings. Renjie is also the author of *Deep into Zabbix*, written in Chinese.

I would like to thank my wife. Only with her devotion to our family was it possible for me to do this excellent job.

www.PacktPub.com

Support files, eBooks, discount offers, and more

For support files and downloads related to your book, please visit www.PacktPub.com.

Did you know that Packt offers eBook versions of every book published, with PDF and ePub files available? You can upgrade to the eBook version at www.PacktPub.com and as a print book customer, you are entitled to a discount on the eBook copy. Get in touch with us at service@packtpub.com for more details.

At www.PacktPub.com, you can also read a collection of free technical articles, sign up for a range of free newsletters and receive exclusive discounts and offers on Packt books and eBooks.

https://www2.packtpub.com/books/subscription/packtlib

Do you need instant solutions to your IT questions? PacktLib is Packt's online digital book library. Here, you can search, access, and read Packt's entire library of books.

Why subscribe?

- Fully searchable across every book published by Packt
- Copy and paste, print, and bookmark content
- On demand and accessible via a web browser

Free access for Packt account holders

If you have an account with Packt at www.PacktPub.com, you can use this to access PacktLib today and view 9 entirely free books. Simply use your login credentials for immediate access.

Table of Contents

Preface   **v**

Chapter 1: Evolution of Zabbix   **1**
  Starting our journey   **2**
  Choosing the right tool   **2**
  The first wrong step with Zabbix   **3**
  Getting started with Zabbix   **4**
  Good practice   **4**
  Simplifying Zabbix   **5**
  Challenges in Zabbix   **6**
  List of don'ts   **8**
    Starting a Zabbix deployment without planning   8
    Use of default templates   8
    Use of default database settings   8
  The beginning of the real challenge   **9**
  Summary   **10**

Chapter 2: Zabbix and I – Almost Heroes   **11**
  After starting Zabbix – the initial steps   **12**
  The natural growth   **13**
  Beyond infrastructure   **16**
  The Internet of Things wave   **16**
  Everyone knows about Zabbix   **19**
  Improvements in Zabbix   **19**
  Talking about performance   **20**
  Summary   **21**

Chapter 3: Tuning the Zabbix Server   **23**
  Item types and performance issues   **24**
    Zabbix data types and SQL fields   26
  Active items – a forgotten option   **27**

Triggers	**28**
Trends and history storage time	**30**
History tables	30
Trend tables	30
Caches and buffers	**32**
Can default templates be the villains?	**34**
DBSyncers – the unknown bottleneck	**35**
Summary	**37**
Chapter 4: Tuning the MySQL Database	**39**
Comparisons between databases	**39**
The main configuration parameters	44
innodb_buffer_pool_size	45
innodb_buffer_pool_instances	45
innodb_flush_log_at_trx_commit	45
innodb_flush_method	46
innodb_log_file_size	46
innodb_io_capacity	46
tmpdir	46
Tuning for reading or writing	**47**
Summary	**48**
Chapter 5: Tuning the Frontend	**49**
The usual complaints	**49**
Differences between web servers	**50**
The main configuration parameters	**52**
Compression in Apache	52
Compression in lighttpd	53
Compression in Nginx	54
Testing compression	**54**
Other alternatives	**55**
Summary	**57**
Chapter 6: Adjusting the Storage	**59**
Choosing between shared and local storage	**59**
Configuring the storage for performance	**63**
Small, medium, or large environments?	**65**
What do I need for my environment?	**66**
Summary	**67**
Chapter 7: Tuning the Operating System	**69**
Linux distributions and Zabbix	**69**
The necessary adjustments in the Kernel	**70**
User-level FD limits	71
Kernel-level FD limits	71

Changing swap behavior	72
Changing IO schedulers	73
The network parameters	76
Summary	**77**

Chapter 8: Doing the Extra Work — 79

Dividing the components	**79**
Specifying the hardware for each component	**81**
Partitioning tables	**85**
Summary	**88**

Chapter 9: Using the Zabbix Proxy — 89

The Zabbix proxy and Zabbix performance	**90**
The first steps with the Zabbix proxy	**92**
The firewall settings	**95**
Hardware for the Zabbix proxy	**96**
Summary	**97**

Chapter 10: Monitoring the Health of Zabbix — 99

The Zabbix queue	**100**
Server and proxy internal items	**102**
Database performance items	**111**
Summary	**112**

Chapter 11: The Next Challenge — 115

Identifying the sponsors of Zabbix	**116**
The demands in business areas	**117**
Developing dashboards	**119**
Zabbix reports	**120**
IT services or SLA reports	**121**
Summary	**123**

Index — 125

Preface

Once, I read a book called *The Outliers* by Malcolm Gladwell. In this book, the author talks about the circumstances that lead people to get certain results in their areas of expertise, whatever they may be—music, sports, math, physics, and so on. The key aim of the author is to assert, based on facts and data, that there are people with extraordinary qualities, but the result depends on the effort, time, and energy devoted to that activity. The opportunity to stand out comes when we are in the right place at the right time. There is a popular saying, "Luck is what happens when capacity/competency and opportunity meet." I think Alexei Vladishev was lucky.

When I met Alexei in 2008, I was surprised by his simplicity and mild nature at the places where he worked, whether it was a training session, a lecture in an auditorium, a meeting with the client, or anything else. He's one of those guys who have in themselves a great guiding force for their actions and decisions, and who don't accept the label of a "pop star" in the open source world. In one of our conversations, he told me about one of the reasons for devoting his professional life to Zabbix SIA and his time to the development of Zabbix—improving people's lives. Simple, and without any "mega" aspiration! He only wanted to help people get their work done better. From this originate his other decisions regarding Zabbix; for example, there is no paid professional or enterprise version.

When I was invited to write this book, I thought about the points I have just described. I thought that it would be a great opportunity to bring to a greater number of people the knowledge that I had gained over the years working with Zabbix in large companies. It would also be a way to give to this field something in return for what I had obtained from it over the years. I hope this book will help you take full advantage of Zabbix, and may it contribute to the goal Alexei had—that of Zabbix being a tool for improving people's lives.

What this book covers

Chapter 1, Evolution of Zabbix, explains that the start with Zabbix is not always glamorous as it does not always have the most advanced features. If you're experiencing performance issues with Zabbix, it is likely that you can solve them without new hardware or software.

Chapter 2, Zabbix and I – Almost Heroes, talks about how Zabbix has evolved due to performance issues in each version. We need to look out for the new features. In this chapter, we also talk about the importance of Zabbix, which grows as the other teams and areas of companies become aware of the potential of this tool.

Chapter 3, Tuning the Zabbix Server, tells you a little more about the possibilities and needs for adjustments to the Zabbix server. It is important to realize that many performance problems can be solved by adjusting the Zabbix server's settings.

Chapter 4, Tuning the MySQL Database, talks about the motivations behind choosing MySQL as the database for Zabbix, and the main MySQL settings related to the performance of Zabbix. In this chapter, you understand a few things about MySQL's behavior with Zabbix.

Chapter 5, Tuning the Frontend, teaches you how to speed up the delivery of Zabbix data to users and improve their experience with the frontend. Nowadays, we can choose from new web servers. Apache is not the sole alternative, nor is it the "killer one."

Chapter 6, Adjusting the Storage, mentions what we must take into account when we think of the hardware, especially the storage to use with Zabbix. To get the best performance from Zabbix, we need to understand how information flows into it and adjust the settings to control the flow of data (reading and writing).

Chapter 7, Tuning the Operating System, considers the fact that the operating system is an important part in this control flow process. We should make sure that we search in our Linux distribution to find the best practices for performance, always taking into account the component that the operating system is involved with (the Zabbix proxy, Zabbix GUI, Zabbix server, or Zabbix database).

Chapter 8, Doing the Extra Work, informs you that it is possible to target the components of Zabbix (the Zabbix server, GUI, and database) on different pieces of hardware. It will also become clear to you that the great hardware consumer is the Zabbix database, and it is this component that must be given the best hardware.

Chapter 9, Using the Zabbix Proxy, proves that the Zabbix proxy can be a powerful ally of the Zabbix server for improving environmental performance. It is good practice to start the environment by already considering a Zabbix proxy, even if it is on the same network in which we have the Zabbix server.

Chapter 10, Monitoring the Health of Zabbix, asserts that Zabbix's internal metrics are an important part of performance tuning. These metrics can't be evaluated alone. We need to understand that they could be affected by other factors, such as the Zabbix database settings.

Chapter 11, The Next Challenge, puts forward a challenge: understanding where and how Zabbix can support the company's business. We should not think of this powerful tool as only something to be used to monitor the IT infrastructure.

The online chapter, *Performance Features and Improvements since Zabbix 1.8*, provides some information about the new features and improvements related to performance since Zabbix 1.8. The chapter is only available online at `https://www.packtpub.com/sites/default/files/downloads/B03410_Appendix.pdf`.

What you need for this book

For this book, you will need good knowledge about Zabbix concepts and administration tasks. We wrote this book to help Zabbix administrators reach new challenges with Zabbix. This book isn't aimed at teaching you how to start a Zabbix deployment; you will need a Zabbix deployment already up and running.

Who this book is for

This book is intended for all Zabbix administrators who, one day, took up the challenge to opt for an open source monitoring tool. This is independent of whether or not you are experiencing performance issues. This book also caters to those who do not want performance problems in the future.

Conventions

In this book, you will find a number of styles of text that distinguish between different kinds of information. Here are some examples of these styles, and an explanation of their meaning.

Code words in text, database table names, folder names, filenames, file extensions, pathnames, dummy URLs, user input, and Twitter handles are shown as follows: "The `innodb_buffer_pool_size` parameter is one of the most important parameters in MySQL."

A block of code is set as follows:

```
...
vm.swappiness = 5
...
```

Any command-line input or output is written as follows:

```
[root]# zabbix_get -s localhost -k kernel.maxfiles
1512039
```

New terms and **important words** are shown in bold. Words that you see on the screen, in menus or dialog boxes for example, appear in the text like this: "Choose the group that the hosts belong to, search for your host, and click on the **Graphs** link."

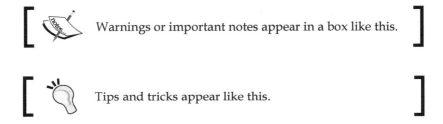

Warnings or important notes appear in a box like this.

Tips and tricks appear like this.

Reader feedback

Feedback from our readers is always welcome. Let us know what you think about this book—what you liked or disliked. Reader feedback is important for us as it helps us develop titles that you will really get the most out of.

To send us general feedback, simply e-mail feedback@packtpub.com, and mention the book's title in the subject of your message.

If there is a topic that you have expertise in and you are interested in either writing or contributing to a book, see our author guide at www.packtpub.com/authors.

Customer support

Now that you are the proud owner of a Packt book, we have a number of things to help you to get the most from your purchase.

Errata

Although we have taken every care to ensure the accuracy of our content, mistakes do happen. If you find a mistake in one of our books—maybe a mistake in the text or the code—we would be grateful if you could report this to us. By doing so, you can save other readers from frustration and help us improve subsequent versions of this book. If you find any errata, please report them by visiting http://www.packtpub.com/submit-errata, selecting your book, clicking on the **Errata Submission Form** link, and entering the details of your errata. Once your errata are verified, your submission will be accepted and the errata will be uploaded to our website or added to any list of existing errata under the Errata section of that title.

To view the previously submitted errata, go to https://www.packtpub.com/books/content/support and enter the name of the book in the search field. The required information will appear under the **Errata** section.

Piracy

Piracy of copyrighted material on the Internet is an ongoing problem across all media. At Packt, we take the protection of our copyright and licenses very seriously. If you come across any illegal copies of our works in any form on the Internet, please provide us with the location address or website name immediately so that we can pursue a remedy.

Please contact us at copyright@packtpub.com with a link to the suspected pirated material.

We appreciate your help in protecting our authors and our ability to bring you valuable content.

Questions

If you have a problem with any aspect of this book, you can contact us at questions@packtpub.com, and we will do our best to address the problem.

1
Evolution of Zabbix

If you are working with Zabbix or any other monitoring tool, you may be knowing a little about downtime costs. Downtime affects companies, products, and even the service's reputation. There is a lot of research that tells us that companies around the world lose a large amount of money because of system outages.

Probably, your company has services or products that depend on IT infrastructure. But the question is: what exactly do you know about these dependencies? Probably a little, but this isn't something that only you missed. Our experience shows that a lot of companies don't know about it.

In this chapter, we will try to explain how Zabbix works in most environments, and the common mistakes we tend to make. We will cover the following topics:

- Starting our journey
- Choosing the right tool
- The first wrong step with Zabbix
- A little about my first steps
- Good practices
- Simplifying Zabbix
- Challenges in Zabbix
- List of don'ts
- The beginning of the real challenge

Starting our journey

Our journey starts when, say, you arrive at work on a sunny Monday (maybe a cloudy day), and your boss is waiting for you in the parking lot. The systems had an outage last night and you need a solution to predict this situation. Now what? Which way to run? Which tool to use? The first step is to try the Internet search engines. Some references will appear—some old, some not so well-known, and so on. But which one should you use? And how to choose the correct tool among so many of them? The specifications and presentations of each one are quite interesting. Apparently, some of them fit into your needs, but which one to use? There are pieces of software, tools, and platforms for all tastes, flavors, and budget sizes. What is your budget? Of course, the lowest possible! Do you have experience with open source? Do you know that the main tools of this type are already professionalized and there are companies that develop and provide support services for these tools? So why not follow this line (gain flexibility and achieve a deployment without exorbitant costs) and work with an open source tool to monitor the environment?

Choosing the right tool

Let's discuss a common scenario. You create a matrix adhesion that lists the main features and defines weights for each. So, beginning the prerequisites and testing the concepts does not take long, and you will realize that Zabbix stands out among all comparative tools. The features are very interesting; Zabbix proves flexible enough to meet all the demands of environmental monitoring. It has an API that allows integration with other systems and applications. You can extract reports regarding recurrence alerts on servers and network assets. It is also possible to have monitoring based on historical data and real-time monitoring. Zabbix works with website monitoring, JAVA, IPMI, SNMP, ODBC, and more. Using Zabbix, it is possible to create rules for servers and other devices to start monitoring without human intervention, that is, automatically. Everything seems to fit the company's needs, and there is a large and active users' community helping and supporting this tool. The tool also has a distributed monitoring model that uses proxies (Zabbix proxy) to ensure data collection even if the monitored environment has no communication with the Zabbix server. Another point to be stressed on is the Zabbix GUI, which is pretty rich and full of possibilities. The developer (Zabbix SIA) has a partnership program supported in many countries and uses the local languages. Why wait more? Some users might say that all the features mentioned so far are present in other tools as well, and in some aspects, they may be even better than Zabbix. So what is the advantage in choosing this tool over others?

From my point of view, Zabbix was born with a very advanced concept compared to other players at that time. I remember my compliance matrix perfectly; there were very important points and impacts on our business model that only Zabbix met.

An example is that the distributed monitoring at that time (version 1.4 of Zabbix) did not have the concept of the Zabbix proxy, but the tool already had the concept of distributed monitoring based on nodes (a functionality that was removed in Zabbix 2.4), and this was something new at that time. Another impact on our business was the ability to segment the environment into a user group and a group of hosts with specific permissions for every requirement (read-only, read-write, and so on).

Here's yet another example—the centralized model that Zabbix always had. In this model, the Zabbix agent is a mere collector, which may or may not gain any intelligence. The alert rules and collection settings are managed and controlled by the Zabbix server, thereby avoiding the need to access the agents when the need for adjusting the collection and alert settings arrives.

Let's get back to the most important items in our business way back in 2007. It's been a few years of learning and development of Zabbix SIA, with the hope of it becoming the best open source monitoring tool. In this sentence lies another great argument for Zabbix: the tool is true open source (in the words of Alexei Vladishev). In various projects in which we participated over the years, it became clear that Zabbix does not leave much to be done by the main commercial monitoring tools, along with the advantage of being open source.

The first wrong step with Zabbix

Another common scenario occurs when the environment created for development, testing, and approval of Zabbix is converted into a production environment.

If the first scenario looked familiar, or at least plausible, this will not be hard to imagine. It is likely that the manager was not waiting for us with a mission and with a big check to be used in the acquisition of hardware and services for the monitoring service. The fact is that this project will often start without many features and without a lot of trust from the rest of the company. In the most common scenario, we begin a test in an environment with restricted servers, and one of the most common mistakes is turning this environment into something that should support all systems and enterprise environments.

Often, Zabbix replaces another monitoring platform that is already in use. In this case, the birth of Zabbix in your environment is more controlled and planned, as there is something existing that you need to replace. But still, another scenario repeats; that is, it uses the same concepts and ideas of the old tool in the implementation of Zabbix. This is another interesting point because users often compare both the tools and lack understanding about Zabbix's features and concepts that ensure correct use of the platform.

These situations can turn into a trap and contribute negatively to the performance of Zabbix.

Getting started with Zabbix

My studies in this wonderful monitoring platform, Zabbix, began in 2005, with the first version of the software. Actually, my experience in monitoring systems dates back to 1994. Since then, I've encountered several tools, commercial and open source, for monitoring IT environments. I admit that open source tools have always been my favorite because of the flexibility that they offer and also because of the developers' ideology. These two points have always guided me in finding and using IT solutions.

When I came across Zabbix in 2005, the platform had not grown enough to be used in our production environments. It started growing from then on, and apparently had good potential. In 2007, with Zabbix version 1.4, we understood that the platform had evolved enough to meet our and our customers' environments. Then we encountered one of the scenarios mentioned in the previous section (using a tool with the concepts of another tool), and faced difficulties in this scenario. The fact is that Zabbix has a learning curve that is a bit steeper than other platforms, because Zabbix's size and the number of features that this platform provides are greater than those of any other technology. Now, challenges will arise because of the large number of features and possibilities with Zabbix, but it grants us fairly wide comprehensiveness in our IT environment. The use of all of these resources without proper planning and understanding of all of Zabbix's components can lead us to a common situation where the monitoring environment will collapse, thus making us abandon the platform.

Good practice

Your environment may have been born in a more controlled and planned manner. You or your staff may have received the correct guidelines, or participated in a training session before starting the deployment of Zabbix in your environment to avoid some inconvenience as the environment grew. However, such cases are rare. My experience shows that first, Zabbix is born out of a desire or requirement of technical teams involved with IT infrastructure, and those responsible for these deployments are solitary heroes who seek a high-level solution with low costs. Often, we do not have the budget to implement this project in our companies. As this monitoring platform shows its value to your company in terms of business, it starts gaining importance and strength. At this point, however, the first challenge arises, because the screen response in the director's or president's office must be an adequate and consistent response to the user's satisfaction (which is quite sensitive in this case).

Simplifying Zabbix

Zabbix's basic objective is data gathering. Basically, this is what Zabbix does. Of course, the collected data will be processed and stored for future comparisons or consultations at regular time periods. The data will also be compared with thresholds (triggers) and viewed by users on screens, maps, and charts. It needs to be cleaned on a routine basis. At this point, things start becoming more complex with Zabbix. Although the platform has a very simple concept (work in data gathering and evaluation), there are factors related to the processing of such data that must be evaluated, and some parameters need to be adjusted to ensure that Zabbix operates properly. This leads to satisfaction of the users and administrators.

In later chapters, we will talk about the concepts and terminology that we define here in this chapter, for your better understanding.

Zabbix was born with its own concepts, terms, and ways of monitoring functions. As you may know, Zabbix was created by Alexei Vladishev in 1998 (in 2001, he published Zabbix's first release). Since the first release, Zabbix has had specific guidelines to work:

- All rules about thresholds, triggers, and alerts are managed by the Zabbix server (not the Zabbix agent).
- Almost all configuration tasks are done at the Zabbix GUI.
- The Zabbix GUI is PHP-based (using a web server and a web browser).
- All of the data (configuration and historical) is stored in a relational database (we are close to storing historical data in a NoSQL database).
- The Zabbix server was developed in the C language (mainly because C has a small footprint).

With this information, we need to start thinking mainly about four Zabbix components: the Zabbix server, Zabbix proxy, Zabbix database, and Zabbix GUI. Each one has its own characteristics and requirements:

- **Zabbix server**: This is the engine — the collector itself — responsible for gathering and/or receiving data from the environment. It is written in the C language and communicates with the Zabbix agents, Zabbix proxy, and Zabbix database. It is the main component of this environment, and manages all the rules (collections, triggers, alerts, and so on).
- **Zabbix GUI**: This is the Zabbix interface where users can see the data gathered by the Zabbix server in the environment. It is written in PHP, uses a web server (supporting PHP), and communicates with the Zabbix database. The Zabbix GUI communicates with the Zabbix server for some minor functions.

- **Zabbix database**: This is the Zabbix data repository. The backend database of Zabbix can be Oracle, IBM DB2, PostgreSQL, MySQL, or SQLite3. In this book, we will cover examples and case studies used with MySQL as the database.

- **Zabbix proxy**: This is an optional component, but as we will see throughout the chapters, when it comes to Zabbix's performance, it is of utmost importance. Its main function is to assist the Zabbix server in data gathering in the monitored hosts. The data gathered by the Zabbix proxy is first kept in a temporary database, and is subsequently sent to the Zabbix server.

These four components create the Zabbix monitoring solution. Throughout this book, we will cover the main aspects related to the performance of each of these components, looking for a clearer and more objective view of the elements and configuration parameters that will directly influence performance.

Challenges in Zabbix

Your challenge starts when you convince your boss that you are responsible for implementing an open source tool to monitor the IT environment for your company. Time progresses and the Zabbix platform starts gaining more and more responsibilities and visibility. However, suppose some important steps were forgotten, or you didn't have all of the information needed to carry out more detailed planning or sizing. The fact is that Zabbix has earned the reputation of an all-seeing eye, and now your company uses Zabbix to support business growth and ensure proper delivery of services.

Since 2007, I have been working with the Zabbix community, and since 2012, I have been a Zabbix certified trainer. In these days, I have heard and seen a lot of guys talking about performance issues with Zabbix. I have no doubt that most of these problems are related to a misconfiguration or misunderstanding about Zabbix's parameters and concepts. Some basic information about Zabbix that people usually don't know or don't care about is as follows:

- **The number of hosts isn't the most important thing for performance**: Usually, people ask, "How many hosts can I manage with Zabbix?" The right question should be, "How many **new values per second** (**nvps**) can I manage with Zabbix?" So, you need to know that one host gathering 100 items is the same as 100 hosts gathering one item each.

- **The default templates shouldn't be used in a production environment**:
It happens that default templates are the only examples that show you how
to use item keys, triggers, graphs, LLD, macros, and other Zabbix features
and functions. Such templates usually have gathering intervals shorter than
what you really need.

- **How many users will use the Zabbix interface**: This is a point that is almost
always forgotten. Usually, people start using Zabbix alone or together with a
few guys, and they have only a few maps and screens. But what if you need
to create a lot of users to use and explore the Zabbix interface? What if your
boss asks you to create some dashboards, putting a lot of data together? At
this point, you'll start to think about web server performance.

- **Using a default database deployment**: The MySQL database comes with
almost all Linux distributions, but my.cnf isn't fit to work with Zabbix.
I mean, the default MySQL deployment isn't the best configuration that
you can work with. Of course, you will need to adjust some basic (maybe
advanced) parameters to attain the best performance with Zabbix. People
don't care about read or write parameters. It's very important to know how
Zabbix works and then prepare your database to work with Zabbix.

- **Item types and value types will directly affect performance**: Do you know
that active items are better than passive items? It's very important to know
that when using active items, the Zabbix server has less work to do, and each
Zabbix agent handles its own queue. Do you know that numerical data is
better than text data? Zabbix uses different tables for each data type (float,
integer, text, log, and so on), and each database table has a different row
configuration.

- **Time retention needs to be shorter than the template's default configuration**:
By default, Zabbix works for 90 days to retain historical data and 365 days
(a year) to retain trends data. Of course, you don't need to retain 90 days of
historical data from an icmp.ping item key. Nor do you need to retain 365
days of trends data from this key. So, you need to choose the right period to
retain your data (historical and trends). You will need to retain some data for a
long time, and you can get rid of the other data earlier.

- **The number of triggers and the functions with them will affect
performance**: Some people don't realize that a trigger with a very simple
function, such as last(), has better performance than a trigger with a more
complex function, such as min(), max(), or avg().

- **Items that are not supported can affect Zabbix's performance**: The Zabbix
server will always try to gather these items, and if they have some error,
the Zabbix server will work without results.

List of don'ts

You need to know some basic things about what to avoid when you start working with Zabbix.

Starting a Zabbix deployment without planning

Lack of planning is the main item in this list of don'ts. Sorry to be repetitive, but if you start a Zabbix deployment without planning, you will have performance issues. So, it is important to know both your environment and Zabbix well.

Use of default templates

Templates that Zabbix SIA sends together with Zabbix are only for testing, and they may be for proving concepts; they are not for use in a production environment. We'll need to create our own templates based on our needs. In the next chapter, you will know that all the default templates are not really meant for you.

Use of default database settings

It doesn't matter which database engine are you using (Oracle, MySQL, pgSQL, or DB2). You will need to change some parameters and tune your database engine. So, you'll need to know about the SQL statements that Zabbix uses and a few more things, as follows:

- How many users will you have? This is precious information to know if you need to tune your database for read or write operations.

- You need knowledge about the hardware. Do you have a storage-backed database? Do you have local disks? How about SAS, SATA, and SSD disks? This is another piece of important information to help you with database tuning.

- Do you have dedicated hardware for the database server? If yes, you can manage the database memory settings (cache and buffer) much better.

- Is this database server a shared server? I mean, is your database server dedicated to the Zabbix database or you have another database together with it? And if you change something to improve Zabbix's performance, will it affect another application?

The beginning of the real challenge

When I started working with Zabbix and deployed our first project with Zabbix, some thoughts that surrounded me were as follows: whether this tool is a reliable one, whether it is possible to use it in large environments, how many users I can have using the Zabbix GUI, and how many hosts or nvps I can manage with Zabbix.

Of course, we started working with Zabbix after a lot of tests and simulations, but a test environment isn't the same as most customers' environments.

In our first project with Zabbix in a large environment (Zabbix version 1.4), we had no Zabbix proxy, caches, or any buffer inside the Zabbix server. Of course, we experienced a lot of troubles regarding performance. We started this project using the Oracle database (because our customer wanted it). After working on this project for some weeks, we began to realize that our performance could be degraded. Our Zabbix GUI was unresponsive, and we were getting some screen errors saying something related to table locks. At such times, the Zabbix database used to execute a lot of SQL update operations in a table called ids. The ids table is very short, with an unexpressive column and row amount. But why did we get these errors? How was Zabbix doing its work?

At this point in time, we asked Zabbix SIA about this behavior. They told us that we had no performance issues with the Zabbix server, but had issues with the Oracle database. We received this information and thought that maybe the application (the Zabbix server) has no performance issues, so let's tune the Oracle database. Therefore, we started working hard on tuning a lot of Oracle parameters. Our Oracle DBAs adjusted all the possible parameters to improve our performance. But we still had performance issues, even though they were few. At this point (2007 to 2008), we were stuck with the project and went back to the planning table.

Our Zabbix-certified guys began a deep investigation to know exactly how (by SQL statements or TCP/IP stack), when (while gathering new values or accessing gathered data), why (to clean-up old data or to create trends data), by whom (the Zabbix server pollers processes or Zabbix server trappers processes), and with how much effort Zabbix will be needed to execute all tasks.

Of course, we have new features nowadays, and it is easier to manage performance. When we started working with Zabbix, we used to read the Zabbix forum threads, looking for a magical solution to our errors. But our environment was not the same, as some specific tuning was made. I mean, zabbix_server.conf, which works like a charm on my environment, can be bad for you.

From the Zabbix forums, it is possible to get a lot of tricks and tips on how to improve Zabbix's performance. Some say they are happy with Zabbix's performance in a large environment and others say they are unhappy with it in a small environment.

But you really need to know about Zabbix's internal tasks, flows, and process. You also need to know about your environment. After using all of this knowledge, you will experience the best monitoring tool you ever knew.

Summary

In this chapter, we saw that the start with Zabbix is not always glamorous and not always start with the most advanced features. The important thing is to realize that planning is the basis of a successful implementation of Zabbix. For reasonable planning, it is important to know the tool reasonably well, and if we are going to plan properly, we must know the tool in great depth.

If you're experiencing performance issues with Zabbix, it is likely that you can solve them without new hardware or software. But for this, you need to know Zabbix, its components, and the possibilities of each. In the next chapter, we will move on to cover this newborn environment, as this is where the majority of people started experiencing performance problems. What happens when everyone wants to use Zabbix? What is the impact of disorderly growth? Let's try to get those answers in the following chapters.

2
Zabbix and I – Almost Heroes

Ever since I started working with IT infrastructure, I have been noticing that almost every company, when they start thinking about a monitoring tool, think of trying to know in some way when the system or service will go down before it actually happens. They expect the monitoring tool to create some kind of alert when something is broken. But by this approach, the system administrator will know about an error or system outage only after the error occurs (and maybe, at the same time, users are trying to use those systems).

We need a monitoring solution to help us predict system outages and any other situation that our services can be affected by. Our approach with monitoring tools should cover not only our **system monitoring** but also our **business monitoring**.

Nowadays, any company (small, medium, or large) has some dependency on technologies, from servers and network assets to IP equipment with a lower environmental impact. Maybe you need security cameras, thermometers, UPS, access control devices, or any other IP device by which you can gather some useful data. What about applications and services? What about data integration or transactions? What about user experience? What about a supplier website or system that you depend on?

We should realize that monitoring things is not restricted to IT infrastructure, and it can be extended to other areas and business levels as well.

In this chapter, we'll cover the following topics:

- Zabbix—the initial steps
- The natural growth
- Beyond infrastructure

- The Internet of Things wave
- Everyone knows about Zabbix
- Things we never thought about
- Talking about performance

After starting Zabbix – the initial steps

Suppose you already have your Zabbix server up and running. In a few weeks, Zabbix has helped you save a lot of time while restoring systems. It has also helped you notice some hidden things in your environment—maybe a flapping port in a network switch, or lack of CPU in a router.

In a few months, Zabbix and you (of course) are like superstars. During lunch, people are talking about you. Some are happy because you've dealt with a recurring error. Maybe, a manager asks you to find a way to monitor a printer because it's very important to their team, another manager asks you to monitor an application, and so on.

The other teams and areas also need some kind of monitoring. They have other things to monitor, not only IT things. But are these people familiar with technical things? Technical words, expressions, flows, and lines of thoughts are not so easy for people with nontechnical backgrounds to understand.

Of course, in **small and medium enterprises** (**SME**), things will go ahead faster and paths will be shorter, but the scenario is not too different in most cases. You can work alone or in a huge team, but now you have another important partner—Zabbix.

An immutable fact is that monitoring things comes with more and more responsibility and reliability. At this point, we have some new issues to solve:

- How do we create and authenticate a user?

    When Zabbix's visibility starts growing in your environment, you will need to think how to manage and handle these users. Do you have an LDAP or Microsoft Active Directory that you can use for centralized authentication? Of course, depending on the users you have, you will have more requests. Will you permit any user to access the Zabbix interface? Only a few? And which ones?

- Is it necessary to create a custom monitor?

  We know that Zabbix has a lot of built-in keys for gathering data. These keys are available for a good number of operating systems. We also have built-in functions used to gather data using the **Intelligent Platform Management Interface (IPMI)**, **Simple Network Management Protocol (SNMP)**, **Open Database Connectivity (ODBC)**, **Java Management Extensions (JMX)**, user parameters in the Zabbix agent, and so on. However, we need to think about a wide scenario where we need to gather data from somewhere Zabbix hasn't reached yet.

  Our experience shows us that most of the time, it is necessary to create custom monitors (not one, but a lot of them). Zabbix is a very flexible and easy-to-customize platform. It is possible to make Zabbix do anything you want. However, to learn every new function or to monitor Zabbix, you'll need to think about what kind of extension you'll use.

- More functions, more data, more load, and more TCP connections!

  This means that when other teams or areas start putting light on Zabbix, you will need to think about the number of new functions or monitors you will need to get. Then, which language to choose to develop these new things? Maybe you know the C language and you are thinking of using Zabbix modules. Will you use bulk operations to avoid network traffic?

The natural growth

In most scenarios, natural growth will occur without control. I mean, people are not used to planning this growth. It is very important to keep it under control.

When some guys start their Zabbix deployment, they probably do not intend to cater to all company teams, areas, or businesses. They think about their needs and their team only. So, they don't think a lot about user rights, mainly because they are technicians and know mostly about hosts, items, triggers, maps, graphs, screens, and so on. What about users who are not technicians? Will they understand the Zabbix interface easily? Do you know that in Zabbix, we have a lot of paths that reach the same point?

The Zabbix interface isn't object-based, which means that users need a lot of clicks to reach (read or write) the information related to an object (hosts, items, graphs, triggers, events, and so on).

If you need to see the most recent data gathered from a specific item, you'll need to use the **Monitoring** menu, then use the **Latest data** menu, choose the group that the host belongs to, choose your host, and finally search for your item in the table.

If you need to see a specific custom graph, use the **Graphs** menu, which is under **Monitoring**. Choose the group that the hosts belong to, choose your host, and then search for your graph in a combobox.

If you need to know about an active trigger in your host, you'll need to use the **Triggers** menu, which is under **Monitoring**. Choose the group that your host belongs to and choose your host. Then, you can see the triggers from that specific host.

If you want to include a new item in an existing custom graph, you'll need to access the **Hosts** menu, which is under **Configuration**. Choose the group that the hosts belong to, search for your host, and click on the **Graphs** link. Then you can choose which graph you want to change.

There are a lot of clicks required to do simple things. Of course, the steps you just saw are something familiar for guys who have deployed Zabbix, but are this true for other teams too?

Maybe, you are thinking right now that it doesn't matter to those guys. But actually, it matters, and it's directly related to Zabbix's growth in your environment. Okay, I think the next two questions will be: are you sure it matters? And why?

Let's agree that the actual Zabbix interface isn't very user friendly for nontechnical guys. But according to the path of natural growth, you started gathering data from a lot of things that are not just IT related. Also, you can develop custom charts and any data from Zabbix via API functions. Now you'll have a lot of nontechnical guys trying to use Zabbix data. I'm sure that it will be necessary to create some maps and screens to help these users get the required information quickly and smoothly.

The following screenshots show how we can transform the viewing layer of Zabbix into something more attractive:

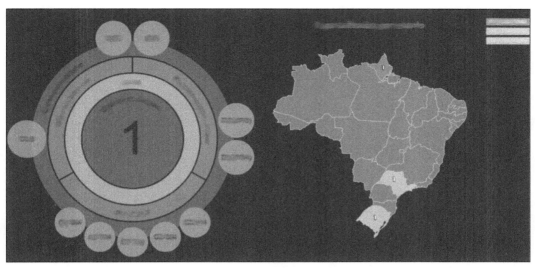

Tactical dashboard

Here is what a strategic dashboard may look like:

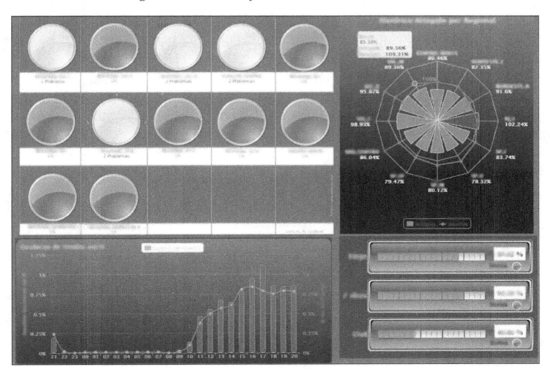

Strategic dashboard

The point here is whether your Zabbix deployment is prepared to cater to these types of requirements.

Beyond infrastructure

I think the monitoring solutions approach is changing, and I like this change. We know that every business nowadays has some dependency on technology, and it is normal to think that a monitoring solution will help keep their systems and services running.

But Zabbix can go beyond this. Actually, any reliable monitoring tool must work like a charm with infrastructure-monitoring things. If a monitoring tool has some loopholes, it's not a good tool and we shouldn't use it.

The real goal of a monitoring solution is how many new methods of gathering data it can show you, and how much it can interact with other tools. Zabbix can do both of these things like a charm.

A few years ago, I worked on a Zabbix deployment created to monitor water pumps. We know that water pumps are not smart devices (at least, the water pumps that I know aren't). That kind of device isn't accessible by a USB or serial port, nor by TCP/IP, SNMP, or any other network protocol. But it was possible to do this; we just needed to find a way to access this kind of device and gather some data.

So, using Zabbix's capabilities and your knowledge about your environment, it is possible to extend monitoring to other business areas. And how many things can you start monitoring? Maybe some business flow? Maybe some door sensors? Maybe the air conditioner's temperature?

The Internet of Things wave

Probably, you have already heard about the **Internet of Things (IoT)**. Just in case you haven't, let me try to explain a little about it.

In 2013, the Gartner Group said that IOTs installed base will grow to 26 billion units by 2020. They also say this:

"By 2020, component costs will have come down to the point that connectivity will become a standard feature, even for processors costing less than 1 USD. This opens up the possibility of connecting just about anything, from the very simple to the very complex, to offer remote control, monitoring and sensing," said Mr. Middleton. "The fact is, that today, many categories of connected things in 2020 don't yet exist. As product designers dream up ways to exploit the inherent connectivity that will be offered in intelligent products, we expect the variety of devices offered to explode."

The **International Telecommunication Union (ITU)** said in 2005:

It looks at the next step in "always on" communications, in which new ubiquitous technologies (such as radio-frequency identification and sensors) promise a world of networked and interconnected devices (for example, fridge, television, vehicle, garage door, and so on) that provide relevant content and information whatever the location of the user — heralding the dawn of a new era, one in which the Internet (of data and people) acquires a new dimension to become an Internet of Things. Topics covered include new enabling technologies, business opportunities, public policy challenges, and implications for the developing world. A statistical annex covering over 200 economies is also included.

But, what exactly is IoT? According to Wikipedia, IoT is as follows:

The Internet of Things (IoT) refers to the interconnection of uniquely identifiable embedded computing-like devices within the existing Internet infrastructure. Typically, IoT is expected to offer advanced connectivity of devices, systems, and services that goes beyond machine-to-machine communications (M2M) and covers a variety of protocols, domains, and applications. The interconnection of these embedded devices (including smart objects), is expected to usher in automation in nearly all fields, while also enabling advanced applications like a smart grid.

According the Beecham Research, our future (and the future comes soon!) will be full of smart devices in many services, sectors, and areas (not only IT):

Service sectors	Application groups/areas
Buildings	• Commercial • Industrial • Institutional
Energy	• Supply/demand • Alternative • Oil and gas
Consumer and home	• Infrastructure • Safety • Convenience • Entertainment
Healthcare and life sciences	• Care • Research
Industrial	• Automation • Processes • Distribution
Transportation	• Non-vehicular • Vehicles • Transport systems
Retail	• Stores • Hospitality • Specialty
Security and safety	• Surveillance • Tracking • Emergency services
IT and networks	• Public • Enterprise

Actually, we have a lot of research and reports from the Gartner Group, Beecham Research, ITU, and others who talk about a near future where all things will be connected to help our businesses.

What about monitoring things? I mean, these kinds of devices, services, and solutions will need some monitoring actions and efforts, won't they? Is your Zabbix server ready to start monitoring these new scenarios?

We definitely need to think beyond IT when we are trying to monitor our business.

Everyone knows about Zabbix

Of course, most teams and user groups know about Zabbix and their capabilities. Will they be asked to create new templates and data collectors? Will they be asked to create new graphs, maps, and screens? You need to realize that your Zabbix server should be prepared to listen to and comply with the user's wishes.

What kind of interaction with Zabbix will the guys from logistics or factory floor have? Surely, you'll receive a lot of tickets asking new questions, and these will come from distinct areas.

Our experience with Zabbix shows that business areas are quite interested in monitoring issues. These are the most demanding users with respect to new monitoring and new ways to visualize the data collected.

These users will not be technical, and that's where we need careful attention. How do we get a collection of data from this diverse environment? Since these users want to visualize this data, a "latest data" screen isn't enough for them. Are the Zabbix maps sufficient for them?

The point to pay attention to is precisely this: be prepared for rapid growth of a monitored environment. We hope this growth will occur in every way, not only in the form of a collection, but also in the ways of displaying this information.

Improvements in Zabbix

Once the things explained here start to happen, we will probably start gathering this new data and create new graphs, maps, and screens. It's normal that our boss or a manager or director will ask us to create new monitoring scenarios *as soon as possible*. Sometimes, we'll forget to plan Zabbix's growth.

Some customers come to us complaining about Zabbix's missed features. Most of these issues can be solved by understanding Zabbix's concepts and configuration parameters.

Of course, Zabbix is a piece of software that is growing every day. Since the 2.0 major version (May 21, 2012), we have had the Zabbix 2.2 major version (November 12, 2013), which introduced more than 100 new features and improvements. We have also had the Zabbix 2.4 major version (September 11, 2014), which comes with at least 50 new features and improvement.

As we are writing this book, the Zabbix SIA teams are planning the Zabbix 3.0 major version. This means that Zabbix is a very active project and each version introduces new features and improvements. Are you up to date with the new features? Do you know whether you are using the new features or not? And how do you know that you didn't miss something?

Sometimes, we forget paying attention to release notes and staying up to date with the latest features and improvements. Maybe, you are getting a bug or some odd behavior. Maybe, this issue has already been solved in a newer version.

Talking about performance

The tabular representation of the new features and improvements related to performance since Zabbix 1.8 can be found in the online chapter, *Performance Features and Improvements since Zabbix 1.8*, which is available at `https://www.packtpub.com/sites/default/files/downloads/B03410_Appendix.pdf`.

According to it, the Zabbix SIA guys are working hard on every Zabbix version to improve performance. I mean, they are thinking about performance and are creating ways to improve it. And how can we stay updated with the enhancements and new features of Zabbix? There are several ways, all of them accessible by and available for any user. The main points of reference are as follows:

- Zabbix's official forum: `https://www.zabbix.com/forum/`
- Zabbix documentation: `https://www.zabbix.com/documentation/2.4/manual/introduction/whatsnew240`
- Zabbix webinars: `http://www.zabbix.com/webinars.php`

Summary

In this chapter, we saw how Zabbix has evolved in terms of performance issues with each version. Also, you realized the importance of the need to be aware of its new features.

Another significant point in this chapter was to realize that the importance of Zabbix is growing, as the other teams and areas of the company are now aware of the potential of this tool. This movement will take Zabbix to all the corners of a company, which often requires a more open approach as far as monitoring tasks is concerned. Monitoring only servers and network assets will not suffice.

The next chapters will feature the most important parameters used to keep our Zabbix environment up and running, with better performance within this scenario that we are designing for Zabbix.

3
Tuning the Zabbix Server

Zabbix is the "all-seeing eye" that gathers data from our environment. The main concept and function of Zabbix is *data gathering in the far corner*. With this understanding, we need to take care of some basic things to help Zabbix achieve its target.

In the previous chapter, we talked about a scenario where Zabbix plays an important role in any environment. Now we need to think about the possible ways to configure Zabbix so that it can achieve the best performance in our environment.

In this chapter, we'll cover the following topics:

- Item types and performance issues
- Active items — a forgotten option
- Triggers matter a lot
- Trends and history storage time
- Is the housekeeper a problem?
- Caches and buffers
- Can default templates be the villains?
- DBSyncers — the unknown bottleneck

Item types and performance issues

As we all know, Alexei Vladishev is the creator of Zabbix. The initial idea dates back to 1998. Zabbix's first alpha and beta releases were launched in 2001 and the first stable version was released in 2004. The following is the historic announcement:

2004/03/23: Zabbix 1.0 available

I'm proud to announce the availability of Zabbix 1.0.

Zabbix is an all-in-one 24 x 7 monitoring solution without high cost. Zabbix is released under the GPL, thus it is free of charge for both commercial and non-commercial use. The full license is available at `http://www.gnu.org/ copyleft/gpl.txt`.

Zabbix can be installed on any UNIX platform. It acts as a server that monitors client systems running on different platforms as well as other network devices. Zabbix has a quick install and can be up and running in less than 15 minutes.

Zabbix's native high-performance agents support virtually every platform including AIX, HP-UX, *BSD, Linux, MacOS, Solaris, and Win32. It also supports SNMP and agentless monitoring, that is, monitoring of simple services such as SMTP, SSH, WWW, FTP, POP3, IMAP, and others without any agent installed on a machine being monitored.

Zabbix offers functionality that will make your IT resources look more transparent, and it will also help to easily identify performance and availability problems. Zabbix greatly increases the productivity of system administrators by providing a simple-to-use monitoring system.

Alexei Vladishev, 2004/03/23

Why am I revisiting this announcement? Because, since this version, there have been a lot of new features and improvements. And this happens in every major or minor version.

Talking about item types and performance, you need to know that each item type has some performance issues you'll need to deal with.

Let's cover a little about item types and how they are gathered:

- The Zabbix agent:
    - This is the most used and popular way to gather data with Zabbix. However, it's an expensive way.
    - A Zabbix poller process (poller is an internal process that work to gather data in remote hosts and servers) will check the next item to be gathered and start working to get this data.

- The Zabbix server starts the TCP connection with the Zabbix agent (port `10050` at the agent side).
- The Zabbix agent (active):
  - This is the best way to gather data with Zabbix. It's not as well known or as commonly used as it should be. Rather, it's a forgotten and unused type.
  - The Zabbix agent asks the Zabbix server for a list of items to send data.
  - The Zabbix agent starts a TCP connection with the Zabbix server (port 10051 at the server side).
  - The incoming connection will be handled by a Zabbix trapper process in this case.
- SNMP (`v1`, `v2c`, and `v3`):
  - SNMP is polled by Zabbix pollers
  - It's an expensive way to gather data
  - Nowadays, it also works with bulk data
  - SNMP `v3` is even more expensive because of authentication and encryption
- SNMP trap and the Zabbix trapper:
  - A trapper process will wait until a device sends new data to the Zabbix server
  - Both of these are fast ways to receive and process new data
- Zabbix aggregate, internal, and calculated:
  - Zabbix aggregate and calculated are internal tools. We have no TCP connections to gather new data. This item type's work with calculations is based on already gathered items.
  - Zabbix internal is also an internal tool. We have no TCP connections to gather new data. This item type's work is to ask internal information to the Zabbix server process.
- Simple check:
  - Simple checks are polled by the Zabbix poller processes
  - The Zabbix server asks the database for the next item to gather data
  - The Zabbix server starts a new TCP connection
  - It is expensive to gather new data

We need to know about each item type to choose the best way to gather the data.

We should also know about the type of information. I mean, thinking about performance, a numeric data type is better than a text or string data type. Of course, this isn't the main point we think about when starting a Zabbix deployment, but we should think about it, especially if we have a large environment. However, it will be a really big problem if our environment gets bigger and bigger.

Zabbix data types and SQL fields

When selecting a data type for a particular item, we need to make sure that it is the correct data type. But, what is the correct data type? Actually, we should consider which data type is the least expensive, considering database writes and reads.

I think we can understand that the database will store each item value in a database table row. After storing, either the Zabbix frontend or another internal process and functions (the housekeeper, trigger evaluation using time shift functions, DBSyncers, actions using macros, and so on) will retrieve this information. These retrieval and write functions cause disk I/O.

Okay. Now let's consider the types of information:

- Numeric (unsigned):
    - Unsigned information is stored in the `history_uint` table
    - This information is stored in a `bigint(20)` unsigned field type
    - It takes 8 bytes to store one value

- Numeric (float):
    - Float information is stored in the history table
    - It is stored in a `double(16,4)` field type
    - It takes 8 bytes to store one value

- Character:
    - Characters are stored in the `history_str` table
    - It is stored in a `varchar(255)` field type
    - It takes up to `length+1` byte to store one value

- Text:
    - Text information is stored in the `history_text` table
    - It is stored in a text field type
    - It takes up to `length + 2` bytes to store one value

- Log:
    - ° Logs are stored in the `history_log` table
    - ° They are stored in a group of fields:

```
Timestamp: int(11)

Source: varchar(64)

Severity: int(11)

Value: text

Logeventid: int(11)
```

As you can see, each item type and information type will affect how data is written in the database. So, you should choose the best one.

Active items – a forgotten option

In the next box, we have a previously made announcement, which is a very important one—the introduction of active checks. Nowadays, people don't recognize the importance of this feature.

2005/05/08: Zabbix 1.1alpha8 released

The release introduces active checks, that is, checks initiated by the Zabbix agent. Using active checks will greatly decrease hardware requirements for the Zabbix server.

I've been holding training sessions since 2009 (I've been an official Zabbix trainer since 2012). In all of those training sessions, when I was talking about the power behind active items, there were some guys getting surprised in almost every session. It happens that the default templates released by Zabbix SIA are created to be easy to try with Zabbix. We shouldn't use these templates in a production environment. We should create our own templates based on them.

The default templates released with Zabbix sources don't use active items. Why? It's too simple and obvious: active items are not so simple to configure. They are not "plug-and-play". Passive items are "plug-and-play", and that is better for new Zabbix users to get to know about Zabbix's features.

Let's think a little about data gathering using the Zabbix agent (with active or passive items). When we are trying to gather some data using the Zabbix agent, we can choose between the Zabbix agent and Zabbix agent (active) item types. Each one has its pros and cons.

Let's say that you have 1,000 hosts and each host has 10 *passive items* for gathering data. In this scenario, the Zabbix server will manage a 10,000 item queue.

Let's say you have 1,000 hosts and each host has 10 active items for gathering data. In this scenario, the Zabbix server will send a 10 item queue to each host.

Of course, it is cheaper to let each Zabbix agent manage a little queue with 10 items than let a Zabbix server manage a huge queue with 10,000 items.

Another goal of active items is to create a buffer on the Zabbix agent side before sending the values to the Zabbix server. In this way, we'll have a lower number of TCP connections. The network managers will thank you for this.

The active agent buffer is very useful in the event of network errors. Your gathered values aren't lost, as in the case of passive items, but the agent will retry to send them.

To know some things more about buffering on the Zabbix agent side, you need to check out the Zabbix agent's configuration file and search for the parameters that are involved with this feature:

- `BufferSend`: This can use values between 1 and 3,600 seconds. By default, the Zabbix agent starts with 5 seconds. In this scenario, it will delay data delivery to the Zabbix server until `BufferSend` reaches its time or `BufferSize` is full. Some environments will be okay with using 10 seconds or higher `values`.

- `BufferSize`: This can use numbers between 2 and 65,535. By default, the Zabbix agent starts with 100 values. In this scenario, it will delay data delivery to the Zabbix server until `BufferSize` is full or `BufferSend` reaches its value.

As you can see, we can reduce the load on the Zabbix server and the TCP connections amount if we start using active items with the Zabbix agent.

What item types are you using? Let's go and change it to start reducing the load on the Zabbix server and network.

Triggers

Trigger functions can also affect the Zabbix server's performance in the same way as items and value types do. We know that Zabbix has a lot of trigger functions and each one has its pros and cons.

Again, the default templates released with Zabbix's sources shouldn't be used in a production environment. Why? That's easy; the trigger functions are really simple and will start lots of events. This amount of events will fill the database tables with unusable or useless data.

On the other hand, we have trigger functions that use time shifting and have a higher processing cost. So, there is a thin line that separates the effectiveness of a trigger and its efficiency.

Basically, we can explain this situation in the following table:

Trigger function	Tolerance	Processing cost
• `last()`: This uses the most recent value (last) received by the Zabbix server	Pretty low for items that frequently change values or receive values that have a huge oscillation, for example, processor load.	The cost is low because the data is dealt at the same time as it arrives at the Zabbix server, and it doesn't make new queries to the database or value cache
• `nodata()`: This uses internal data to calculate the time since the last gathered value and the delay	Average for items that are subject to timeout due to high network latency.	Low cost because it works with unique and punctual data (`last_clock` and `delay`)
• `min()` and `max()`: These use gathered and stored data from the history table	Variable, depending on the parameter defined for the time or quantity of gathers. Usually, it generates a small number of alerts.	Average to high, depending on the parameter defined for the time or quantity of gathers
• `avg()`: This uses gathered and stored data from the history table	Average to low, depending on the parameter defined for the time or quantity of gathers.	Average to high, depending on the parameter defined for the time or quantity of gathers

We explained only a few trigger functions so that you can get an initial understanding that a chosen function can change the trigger sensitivity, making it more or less sensitive (affecting the number of events and therefore increasing the amount of data in the database tables); alternatively, the function can affect the performance of the Zabbix server according to the way the values will be assessed.

For a better understanding of trigger functions, refer to the Zabbix manual at `https://www.zabbix.com/documentation/2.4/manual/appendix/triggers/functions`.

Our challenge will be to create triggers with the correct sensitivity and lowest processing costs.

Trends and history storage time

Let's cover another important point that is, at times, forgotten by Zabbix administrators. Differently from other monitoring tools, Zabbix allows each item to have its own time for data holding configured individually. There are two ways for this to occur.

History tables

Zabbix works with five history tables, two of which are used to store numerical data (`history` and `history_unit`).

Each item can have its own retention time defined in the `History storage period` field (in days). This period defines the maximum amount of time (in days) that the collected values from the particular item will remain in the database.

After this period, an internal process called housekeeping will remove the old data from the database. This function creates concurrency competition for reading and writing. At this point, the housekeeping tool needs to select the data that will be erased and also issue `DELETE` SQL statements that will be generated to eliminate this data.

Trend tables

Like history tables, it is also possible to set a maximum retention time for each item in trend tables, which are actually a consolidation of data from history tables.

Every hour (00:00, 01:00, 02:00, 03:00, and so on), an internal function of the Zabbix Server accesses the history tables that store numerical data and aggregates the data from the last hour. This process will generate a new row in the trends table with the consolidated data. The `trend storage period` directive (in days) will set the retention time of this item in the trend tables.

With this in mind, we can understand that we can work with two retention settings for the items. The following is the impact of this function when talking about Zabbix's performance:

- We will have an item with a gathering time (update interval delay) of 60 seconds. This setting will generate 60 values (or rows) in the history tables in 1 hour. Each row needs approximately 90 bytes.

- Every hour (00:00, 01:00, 02:00, 03:00, and so on), Zabbix will aggregate the 60 values it has received in one unique row in the trends table. Each row has about 128 bytes. The composed row is made up of four values: min, max, avg, and num (count). The next figure shows you how trends work:

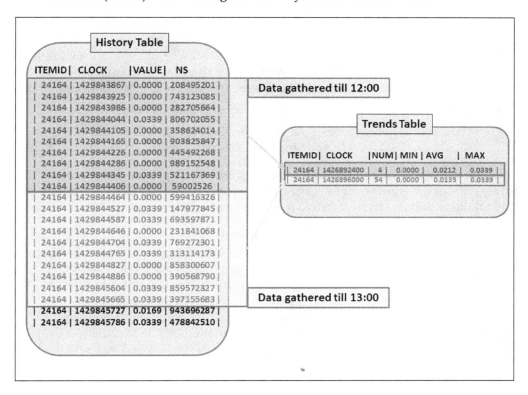

Once more, default templates are the villains in our scenario. This is because they, as a standard, have a retention time of 90 days for history tables, and 365 days for trends tables.

The question here is: do we need to keep the collected data for so long? Probably not, and we can use different times for specific data.

Caches and buffers

In the early versions of Zabbix up to version 1.6, all Zabbix server interaction with data occurred directly via SQL statements in the database. For collecting an item, the flow was as follows:

- The Zabbix server queried the database in search of the next item to be gathered (which would, actually, be the latest item for collection)
- This query basically took into account two fields in the items table (`delay` and `last_clock`)
- If the duration of the gap between the current time and `last_clock` (time of the last valid sample collection) was greater than `delay` (number of seconds between gathers), then the Zabbix server started a new collection for that item
- A poller would be called and the collection would be made
- When this poller received data from the Zabbix agent, it would execute `INSERT` on the database and store the collected values

The entire collection stream involved querying and writing (insert and update) to the database. In an environment of a large organization, where we have thousands of hosts and tens of thousands of items, it is possible to understand that the bottleneck would undoubtedly be in the database.

For the purpose of comprehensiveness and understanding, we should add to that environment triggers and their functions, the housekeeper, the Zabbix frontend, users' actions, alerts and escalations, and so on. The important fact is that the database has ended up being the main point when talking about Zabbix's performance. Zabbix SIA came to the conclusion that Zabbix should minimize its interactions with the database, or have these interactions be executed in the background by new internal processes and structures (caches and buffers).

Zabbix version 1.8 introduced some caches and buffers, which kept evolving. Today, they are responsible for ensuring good performance. Currently, the main caches and buffers are as follows:

- `CacheSize` (configuration cache):
    - This stores all configuration data (hosts, items, and triggers)
    - It has a minimum value of 128 KB and a maximum value of 8 GB
    - If the volume of configuration data is larger than the size of `CacheSize`, the Zabbix server will not launch

- ○ The Zabbix server will stop if the configuration cache becomes full at runtime
- ○ This cache is stable and must be monitored so that its capacity stays between 80 and 90 percent

- `HistoryCacheSize` (history cache):
  - ○ This stores the data received by the Zabbix server, pollers, or trappers
  - ○ It has a minimum value of 128 KB and a maximum value of 2 GB
  - ○ If it is completely filled, the Zabbix server starts rejecting new values
  - ○ This is a security cache and will only grow if the Zabbix server has difficulties delivering data to the database
  - ○ It must be monitored so that it remains as empty as possible (it may fluctuate due to writing database disk latency)
  - ○ It keeps the highest possible value (2 GB) so that there is no gathering queue at times when the database/storage is slower

- `HistoryTextCacheSize` (history text cache):
  - ○ This has the same function and behavior as `HistoryCacheSize`. However, it receives data items of only three kinds: characters, text, and log.

- `ValueCache` (value cache):
  - ○ This was introduced in version 2.2. It is used to make calculations of trigger expressions, calculated/aggregate items, and some macros much faster.
  - ○ It has a minimum value of 128 KB (`0` disables `ValueCache`) and a maximum value of 64 GB.
  - ○ It grows gradually as more values are added to it.
  - ○ It must be monitored to ensure that its values increase (if there is memory available) in the event of being full.

- `TrendCacheSize` (trends cache):
  - ○ This is used to store trends data before writes to the database.
  - ○ It has a minimum value of 128 KB and a maximum value of 2 GB.
  - ○ It doesn't change much. It depends on the number of items.

With these settings, we can eliminate much of direct access to the database.

The main point here is to establish adequate monitoring of these caches and buffers so that we know how they are behaving and whether they need some adjustments in the parameter values assigned. For example, if `HistoryCache` and/or `HistoryTextCache` fluctuate a lot, this indicates that the Zabbix server has difficulties in delivering data to the database. The bigger this cache, the longer the Zabbix server supports this fluctuation.

To learn more about internal items related to caches and buffers inside Zabbix, take a look at the Zabbix manual and stay up to date with new keys and parameters.

In short, we must understand and exploit Zabbix's caches and buffers so that we can manipulate data in the storage and minimize database access.

Can default templates be the villains?

Without a doubt, default templates are the villains. Surprised?

So far, we have talked about the characteristics of items and triggers, and how small adjustments (collection times, retention time, data types, function triggers, and so on) can save a Zabbix deployment from failure.

How do Zabbix's standard templates come to us? Have you stopped to think whether they are designed with the best practices for a production environment in mind? Many Zabbix users start using the software without this in mind and end up compromising the success of Zabbix in their environments.

Here's what should we know, and most likely change, before starting to use Zabbix:

- Default templates and items:
    - The update intervals are very short and do not consider the requirements of each environment
    - The retention times are standardized for all items (90 days for history and 365 days for trends), and it is certainly not necessary for the retention time for all items to be the same
    - Zabbix's default templates don't use user macros
- Default templates and triggers:
    - Triggers in default templates don't use user macros.
    - They use very sensitive functions, which can generate too many events. These increase the amount of data in the tables.
    - Triggers in default templates aren't configured to use dependencies (another way to minimize unnecessary events).

The conclusion is that the standard templates of Zabbix are easy to use, especially when we are starting an implementation of Zabbix and we need speed so that the environment can be set up quickly. However, these templates are a trap, and problems begin to emerge a few months (or weeks) after we have started working with Zabbix. So, we should not use the default templates in a production environment. Some of you will ask: why does Zabbix SIA provide these templates if they should not be used? The answer is simple: so that we can have a fast start as a proof of concept or testing with the platform.

DBSyncers – the unknown bottleneck

With the introduction of caches and buffers (in Zabbix version 1.8), it was necessary to create an internal process that could control the data entering and leaving these caches and buffers. In practice, we have two processes responsible for data management:

- Configuration syncer:
    - This process manages the cache of configuration data.
    - It's a unique process (it is neither necessary nor possible to increase the amount of syncer).
    - The time of the sync data is controlled by the CacheUpdateFrequency parameter (zabbix_server.conf). By default, this time is set to 60 seconds.

- History syncer:
    - This writes the gathered data to the database
    - As a standard, we have four processes that can (and usually should) be changed to a higher or lower value, depending on the necessity and limitations of the environment
    - The syncing time for the data gathered is 5 seconds for each DBSyncer, and it can't be changed by the user
    - The number of DBSyncers is controlled by the StartDBSyncer parameter (zabbix_server.conf) and is limited to 100

Our focus here is on the DBSyncers, and I think that at this point, it is already clear what happens when the database is restraining or slowing down the writing—the DBSyncers will take longer to perform their task and get all of them busier. Hence, the history cache passes will retain more values. In this scenario, the most common symptoms are as follows:

- High occupancy of the DBSyncers
- High occupancy of the history cache (which should be empty or almost empty—always)
- Another important symptom is gaps in graphs, which are filled with some delay

So, in an initial evaluation, if we have these symptoms, it means that the database is not handling the gathered data, and we should think of better hardware for the database. Right? This is actually incorrect because there is another possibility, which is not always evaluated but is common in large environments.

Let's imagine that we have these symptoms (DBSyncers and history cache are constantly busy) and we are sure that our database and storage can handle 10 times per second the values we are collecting right now. That's easy! Zabbix is limited and does not have scalability to the size of my environment. Correct? In fact, it's wrong again.

In the aforementioned scenario, it is most likely necessary to increase the number of DBSyncers to a greater value (8, 12, 20, and so on) so that we can have more processes taking data from the cache to the database. In large environments, this scenario usually repeats itself and administrators are unaware of the Zabbix function and possible DBSyncers configurations. But we can't just drastically increase the number of DBSyncers, let alone set this value to the maximum possible (100 cases). We should monitor the occupation of these processes and increase the amount gradually as required. Otherwise, we can create more problems than solutions. An uncontrolled increase in this parameter can have a very negative impact on the database.

Be sure to immediately start monitoring the DBSyncers' history and cache activity. With this information, you can identify Zabbix's behavior and adjust the number of DBSyncers so that it fits your environment.

To clarify a bit more about the DBSyncers, see the following screenshot. In it, you can see what the relationship of each of these processes with each cache and buffer is:

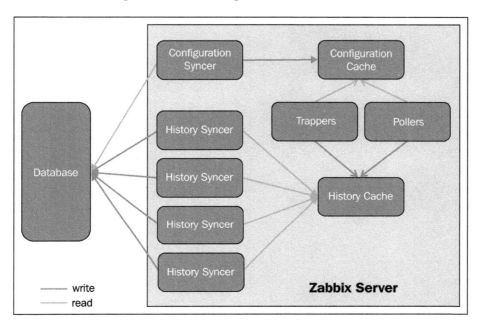

Summary

In this chapter, you got to know a little more about the possibilities of, and need for adjustments to the Zabbix server. It is important to realize that many performance problems can be solved by adjusting the Zabbix server's settings.

Also, it has been seen that since version 1.8, Zabbix SIA seeks to control the flow of data by manipulating information in caches and buffers to minimize the need for reading and writing to the disk. So, we need to control the main configuration parameters related to caches and buffers. Another relevant point is related to the default templates that Zabbix uses. This practice should be avoided, or else it may cause performance issues in medium and large environments. This is also no less important: we have information about data retention time and the types of items. These settings directly affect environmental performance.

In the next chapter, we will discuss the main MySQL configuration parameters that are directly related to the performance of Zabbix.

4
Tuning the MySQL Database

So far, we have talked about the settings of the Zabbix server and its internal components. Also, you learned how Zabbix's caches and buffers minimize the database hardware requirements. But we must be attentive to the database's performance settings. I often say that the correct database configuration is one of the keys to success in a Zabbix implementation. Administrators often simply define the Zabbix database and start using Zabbix, without making the adjustments necessary for good performance. In this chapter, we will talk about these topics:

- Comparisons between databases
- Why choose MySQL?
- The main configuration parameters
- Tuning for reading or writing

Comparisons between databases

To understand why MySQL is the most widely used database within Zabbix and why Zabbix SIA tends to use MySQL (for main development and ready-to-use appliances) instead of other RDBMS, you need to know some details about the supported databases and the main characteristics directly related to Zabbix.

According to the Zabbix manual at `https://www.zabbix.com/documentation/2.4/manual/appendix/performance_tuning`, Zabbix SIA has good support for MySQL.

This topic does not offer a comparison to determine which the best database is, but a comparison to understand which database has the best behavior with the Zabbix platform. The difference in approach is important so that you can have an assessment free of any bias, positive or negative, regarding any of the databases supported by Zabbix.

We know that the Zabbix server and the Zabbix proxy natively support five databases:

- Oracle
    - 10g or later
    - Commercial license

- IBM DB2
    - 9.7 or later
    - Commercial license

- PostgreSQL
    - 8.1 or later
    - BSD license
    - It is recommended to use at least 8.3 (which introduced much better vacuum performance)

- MySQL
    - 5.0.3 or later
    - The InnoDB engine is required
    - GPL and commercial license

- SQLite3
    - 3.3.5 or later
    - Public domain license
    - It's not recommended to be used with the Zabbix server
    - It's the best option to be used with the Zabbix proxy

Each database has its own characteristics, facilitators, and factors to be considered when used with Zabbix. But the focal points here are as follows: what does Zabbix need from the database? And how does Zabbix handle the data and how it impacts the database?

Let's think a bit about the data stream in Zabbix so that you can get a better understanding of how the database is used.

Since Zabbix version 1.8, a lot of caches and buffers have been implemented, which have greatly improved the processes of reading and writing data. With this feature, the load on the database became smaller and the impact, if any contingency in the database, was also reduced.

In a typical Zabbix environment, which SQL statement occurs more— SELECT, INSERT, UPDATE, or DELETE—on the database? In the current versions of Zabbix, we perform more SELECT and DELETE operations. In the next two screenshots, you can see how a medium-sized (~500 values per second and ~15 concurrent users online) Zabbix server works with a MySQL database:

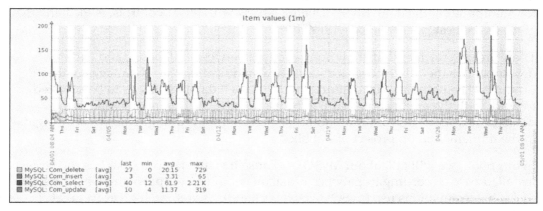

1-month's MySQL operations

The following screenshot shows the average operations per week across a month:

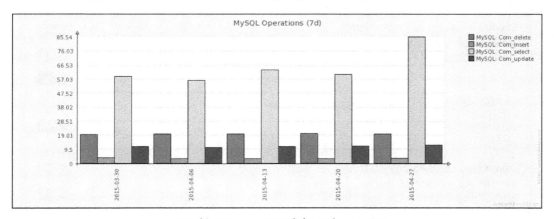

1 month's average per week for each operation

This behavior may be different in environments that have scenarios far beyond the scope of the *standard*. But what is the standard? What is a typical environment? Well, I'm considering an environment where nothing is greatly exaggerated.

Zabbix environments may vary. It depends on the number of users, screens, maps, collection type and data type, and so on. I'm bringing up information considering a typical balanced environment.

How does each database behave and fit into this scenario? What are the characteristics of each database we should consider when deciding which one to use?

Basically, we need a database that will grant us greater speed of reading and writing the data being manipulated by Zabbix. This point goes through the controls that each database has on the data. In theory, the more control we have, the more the overhead for manipulating the data. MySQL, being a bank with fewer controls, is the bank that gives us the best performance with Zabbix.

There are several sites that show comparatives between databases, and each developer has their own comparatives, always indicating the advantages of their products. The point here is to understand that each database needs to be adjusted to work with the application that will be used in the environment. None of the databases supported by Zabbix should be used without tuning. This is a very big risk in the implementation project of Zabbix.

In our book, we will talk about MySQL because it is the database that has the largest installed base (according to Zabbix's Brazilian community, approximately 81 percent of Zabbix installations use MySQL as the backend). Therefore, it gives us greater authority to write about it.

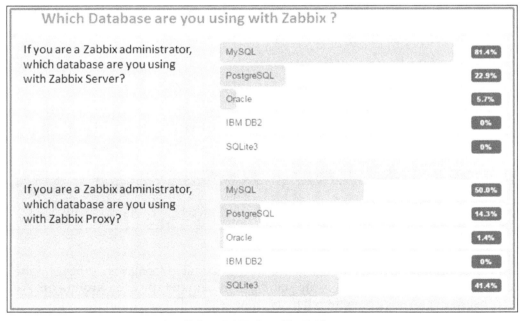

A poll about RDBMS used by Zabbix users

It is quite important to note that PostgreSQL is growing to become as good an alternative as RDBMS to use with Zabbix server. Performance problems (such as excessive locks) with older versions no longer exist. The latest versions of PostgreSQL (at the time of writing this book, the latest version is 9.4) can be used without any worry about performance. This is provided, of course, you make the necessary performance adjustments to Zabbix.

Zabbix SIA tells us that we should use the database that our company has more knowledge of. This means that if our experience is greater with Oracle, or we have a team dedicated to Oracle, this is the database that we should use. This rule applies to any database supported by Zabbix. But, in practice, it is a little different because database administrators don't always know the application, or aren't always interested in knowing it, which is needed in order to do the best performance tuning. Also, we must say that Oracle (a bit older than DB2) and IBM DB2 support for Zabbix is a recent occurrence, and maybe this fact can lead to less tested and optimized environments.

What we see is that many database administrators perform standard tuning on the database, which does not guarantee better performance. In this scenario, MySQL has this advantage as it is one of the most popular databases used worldwide. There are many sites, blogs, and forums that talk about MySQL's performance. We should also consider some important points in favor of MySQL:

- MySQL is the database used by Zabbix SIA for the development of Zabbix. The SQL statements are first created in MySQL and then written to other databases.
- MySQL is the most widely used database with Zabbix worldwide. We get much more information from Zabbix with MySQL than with other databases.
- Reportedly, MySQL is developed with an emphasis on speed, leaving aside the lesser used features.

I believe that these points are relevant when deciding which database to use with Zabbix.

We have a good testimony from a Zabbix user who chose Oracle instead of MySQL:

> *I used Oracle in the early time of 2011. When I found some performance issues with Oracle, I read Zabbix source code, which is used to talk with databases and found some code written to maximize the performance of MySQL. But unfortunately, with these features, Oracle cannot achieve its best point. What I can remember now is a feature that Zabbix will make a large SQL by putting a set of small SQL in a process of beginning and ending. This will impact Oracle's performance because of something like shared cursor. What I did to fix this was to split this large SQL to small SQL. In fact, I think the Zabbix development team has tested Zabbix under MySQL and MySQL is recommended by Zabbix. (Zabbix user, Baniu Yao)*

For those interested in comparisons, this list provides some references:

- `http://arxiv.org/ftp/arxiv/papers/1205/1205.2889.pdf`
- `http://www-css.fnal.gov/dsg/external/freeware/mysql-vs-pgsql.html`
- `http://www.wikivs.com/wiki/MySQL_vs_PostgreSQL`
- `http://it.toolbox.com/blogs/oracle-guide/oracle-10g-vs-postgresql-8-vs-mysql-5-5452`
- `http://troels.arvin.dk/db/rdbms/`
- `https://blogs.oracle.com/GeorgeTrujillo/entry/mysql_versus_oracle_features_functionality`

Also, it should be mentioned that when we are talking about MySQL, we are talking about all MySQL variants and forks (Percona Server, Drizzle, MariaDB, and so on).

The main configuration parameters

Now, we will talk about the main MySQL configuration parameters that must be known and considered in a Zabbix deployment. Each parameter should really be understood so that we know the correct settings for the scenery. In assessing the need for adjustments to the parameters mentioned here, we should consider the hardware we're using for MySQL. It is important to remember that there is no cake recipe that works for any environment. We need to know and consider our variables before applying any changes to the database. Here, we consider that users have a good knowledge of the database and the consequences of a misconfiguration. Also note that we always keep an updated backup to restore in case it is needed.

Ever since I started my projects with Zabbix, I have heard and read a lot about tuning the database. One of the oldest and most discussed tips is table partitioning. Here, we have a very important point because this change in the database requires special care when, for example, migrating to a new version. The issue is that in the forums, whenever we find a miraculous tip to improve the performance of the database, we cannot estimate to what extent this foolproof recipe will work in our environment. To the surprise of many, a copy-and-paste action in a configuration that worked like a charm for a forum user can sometimes worsen your environment.

So, remember that there is no magical configuration file that can be used in any MySQL server that acts as a backend for Zabbix. This is the most common error and has a great impact on the performance of Zabbix.

In the following sections, I have tried to provide information about the main database configuration parameters related to the performance of Zabbix. The intention is to know in which situation they should or should not be used.

Since we are using InnoDB as the engine for the database tables, we must consider and know these parameters (`my.cnf`).

innodb_buffer_pool_size

The `innodb_buffer_pool_size` parameter is one of the most important parameters in MySQL. In reality, it is the memory space we are dedicating to MySQL to work with the data from the InnoDB tables. The higher this value, the better Zabbix will perform. The main point is that the appropriate value should not generate problems, rather provide solutions.

If we are working with dedicated hardware for the database, it is easier to set this parameter to the optimal. Some sites tell us to use this parameter at 80 percent of the available physical memory. For example, if we have 1 GB of physical memory, we can set 800 MB as `innodb_buffer_pool_size`.

innodb_buffer_pool_instances

A little known, and therefore not widely used, parameter is `innodb_buffer_pool_instance`. In practice, it is the possibility of having multiple buffer pool instances working together to minimize memory contention access to memory areas when using 64 bit systems and a large value for `innodb_buffer_pool_size`. What can happen is that many threads accessing the same instance buffer pool can lead to conflict in the database.

The proper way here is to use one `innodb_buffer_pool_instance` parameter for every 1 GB of memory in `innodb_buffer_pool_size`. That being said, if we have 8 GB in the buffer pool size, we should use `innodb_buffer_pool_instances = 8`.

innodb_flush_log_at_trx_commit

With the `innodb_flush_log_at_trx_commit` parameter, we tell MySQL what the balance between ensuring the recording of the data (commit operations) and the high performance required for Zabbix is.

By default, MySQL has the value 1 (strict ACID compliance), which means that the contents of `log_buffer` will be written to the log for each commit, and then the log will be flushed to the disk.

The trick is to use 0 for this parameter. With this change, the log value will be flushed to the disk every second (approximately), which creates a risk of data loss in the event of MySQL crashing. For Zabbix, I think this risk can be assumed without further concerns, but we need to consider it in favor of performance. Each user should evaluate their needs and decide whether or not to take that risk. In this case, we'll have less I/O and, consequently, quicker write operations.

innodb_flush_method

The `innodb_flush_method` parameter controls the method used to flush data to the data files and log files. The `set` method directly affects the I/O throughput, but this parameter is considered only on the Unix and Linux operating systems.

By default, MySQL uses the `fsync` method, which uses the `fsync()` system call to flush the data to the log files.

When using this with Zabbix, we should consider using the `O_DIRECT` value. In this case, MySQL will use the `O_DIRECT` system call to open the data files and the `fsync()` system call to flush both (data and log files).

innodb_log_file_size

The `innodb_log_file_size` parameter controls the size of each log file (by default, it is two files).

The bigger the value, the bigger the economy we have with respect to the I/O. But the bigger the value, the slower will be the recovery from a crash.

To determine the value, we must know the behavior of MySQL (with Zabbix) in our environment. There is no direct way to establish this value. Some sites have formulas and tips on how to find the best value. The reality is that the default value (48 MB) is very low, so we need to adjust it for our environment. We can start with 512 MB, then 1 GB, then 2 GB, and so on.

innodb_io_capacity

The `innodb_io_capacity` parameter controls the I/O limit used by the InnoDB tasks. The default value is `200`, and it should be changed so that it can be used with Zabbix, especially in large environments.

The proper value is the closest to the physical limit of the hardware being used. In SSDs for example, we can adjust this value to `2000` or `3000`. For SAS disks, it should be about `500` or `1000` (depending on the amount of disks and RAID, if used).

tmpdir

The `tmpdir` is where MySQL will create the necessary `temp` tables during the operations that require such tables. One tip is to adjust this value for a memory area (usually `/dev/shm`).

Since MySQL version 5.5, we have an important point in this configuration because `tmpfs` doesn't support AIO (asynchronous I/O). The question we need to ask is: "What is the best in terms of performance for Zabbix?"

Tuning for reading or writing

This is a question that we don't always ask, but it is important when we have a large environment and lots of users accessing Zabbix's frontend.

Most of the time, we worry only about performance so that we can meet all the VPS that Zabbix needs (tuning for writing), but we must not forget that we will have users accessing the frontend to read the data that was collected (tuning for reading).

The main point here is that we should understand our environment so that we can think about the tuning we need to perform in MySQL.

The more users we have in Zabbix, the more read operations that the database will run. For example, to access a screen that contains graphics and a map with 50 hosts participating in five groups, Zabbix needs to do the following:

- Validate user permissions for each of the host groups existing in the map
- Search for information about each host in the map
- Search for information about the triggers and events on each host
- Validate graphics permissions (host and host group)
- Search for information (items history) about each of the graphics

Now, let's imagine that we have dozens of screens, maps, and users in Zabbix. Also consider that we have the screens of the NOC (short for network operation center), with a screen refresh every 2 or 3 minutes. Take into consideration that the housekeeping will select the data to be deleted from the database. We also have the internal functions working (select and insert) to aggregate data into trends tables.

Another important fact is that the Zabbix GUI does not work with any cache or buffer, and it needs to access the database directly.

In a typical Zabbix implementation, we will have more reading (select) than writing (insert, update, and delete) operations.

Another detail, often forgotten or overlooked, is the fact that Zabbix performs many small queries. Therefore, the MySQL query cache can be disabled because the cost of managing such cache is sometimes larger than running these queries without cache. We must also consider that many queries executed by Zabbix consider the date and time (minutes and seconds), which does not favor the use of a cache for queries. So, it is possible (but not fully recommended) to disable the query cache by adjusting the following parameters:

- `query_cache_size=0`
- `query_cache_type=0`

Summary

In this chapter, you understood a few things about MySQL's behavior with Zabbix.

What we need to keep in mind is that we need to know (or design) our environment and take into account the number of Zabbix users, the number of screens and maps created, the number of VPS necessary, the database disks (SSD, SAS, SATA, and so on), and the database's physical memory (for the `innodb_buffer_pool_size` configuration).

The more we know about the environment, the easier it will be to define the correct parameter of our MySQL.

We also talked about the reasons for choosing MySQL as the database for Zabbix and the main MySQL settings related to Zabbix's performance. In the next chapter, we'll talk about the Zabbix frontend and how this part can be handled for better performance.

5
Tuning the Frontend

There is an important character in scenarios where Zabbix is used — the user. The perception of this character can compromise the deployment. If Zabbix's frontend doesn't have adequate performance or is slow in loading screens, it doesn't matter how many **values per second** (**VPS**) our Zabbix server is managing to process, because you get a negative experience when trying to access data. The aim of this chapter is to take a look at this component of Zabbix (frontend) and seek the best alternative web servers and settings for any software. In this chapter, we are going to talk about:

- Things users usually complain about
- Differences between web servers
- Main configuration parameters
- Other alternatives

The usual complaints

Generally, when we start using Zabbix, only the technicians who have installed Zabbix and are working as supporters for the environment have access to the frontend. But after a while, others will have access to the Zabbix frontend. So, the frontend performance will be tested and required much more than before.

As we already know, users can do amazing things with the software — things that developers cannot even think of during development. For example, in each user's profile configuration, it is possible to change their own settings:

- Language
- Theme
- Auto-login

- Auto-logout (minimum 90 seconds)
- Refresh (in seconds)
- Rows per page
- URL (after login)

Well, where is the risk with these settings? You may have noticed that the risk is in **Refresh** and **Rows per page**. If the user decides to change **Refresh** to **5** and **Rows per page** to **10,000** then what will happen? We will have a problem—a user complaining that Zabbix screens are too slow to load.

Another point is the fact that we will create maps, screens, slide shows, and graphics. Each of these components needs to read host data, triggers, items, and so on. The more maps, screens, and graphics, the more data is delivered to users at all times. At this point, the frontend becomes really necessary.

What do users often complain about? Of course, slow loading of Zabbix screens. In practice, all screens that require user validation (that is, almost all Zabbix screens) will use more resources, especially if we have a lot of users and host groups. This can cause a big problem. In Zabbix version 2.2, there was a change in the permission validation algorithm. This was done to minimize the impact of validation on screens. Until version 2.2 of Zabbix, we had a piece of logic for validation of permissions where it was necessary to validate all user groups to see whether the user had denied access to some of them to the host group. From version 2.2 onwards, this logic was changed, and Zabbix started to validate user access to data from a host in the first group where the user had permission to participate but not pass through other groups. This made Zabbix faster when validating permissions.

Going back to user complaints, we have other complaints, such as delays in assembling data in a graph or access to available reports. The fact is that the web server can directly impact the delivery of data to users.

We need to think and understand how to read and deliver data faster to users.

Differences between web servers

I remember the time when the most widely used software in e-mail servers around the world was Sendmail. Today, we have Postfix in this position (with Exim growing and qmail being discontinued). Sendmail is hard to administrate and falls short in performance. Postfix is easy to administrate and performs well.

But why are we talking about Sendmail and Postfix in a frontend chapter? Because I want to touch on a point of relative importance to Zabbix, which is the choice of the best web server for the task of delivering the collected data to Zabbix users.

With Zabbix, history repeated itself. There was a time when we thought only of Nagios when it came to open source monitoring platforms. Today, Zabbix has taken that position in many countries.

The point is that new platforms emerge to perform the same tasks in a simpler and more efficient way. Why would it be different with the web server? For a long time, Apache was the best and most widely used solution for web servers. Has this scenario changed? Not yet, but we have clear signs that we are on the way to a change.

Undoubtedly, at the time of writing this book, Apache is the most used web server in the world (http://w3techs.com/technologies/overview/web_server/all), and has contributed much to the growth of the Internet since its inception. But today, we have good and interesting alternatives such as Nginx, Cherokee, and lighttpd. Which of these is the best option to use with Zabbix?

Let's try to understand a little about Apache, Nginx, and lighttpd, which are the most commonly used web servers with Zabbix. Apache is based on threads, and for each new thread, a connection is started and it consumes more memory. Nginx and lighttpd work a little differently and have a unique process that manages all connections. Basically, we have in the use of resources (especially memory) a big difference between these three web servers. Of course, there are other differences that can impact other applications, such as the number of available modules. But for Zabbix, these three web servers have everything you need. In Nginx and lighttpd, PHP is accessed directly (php-fpm and FastCGI). This already brings gains since it is a single process (and there are few threads). It will take up fewer resources in the operating system.

Are there real differences between the use of one web server and another? In practice, yes, because with less use of resources, the more *modern* web server will support more requests. But will it have a better response? This is where some controversy may arise, because even though Apache consumes more resources, it remains powerful and full of possibilities. Testing in your environment (considering the required load and the hardware) is worthwhile to understand which web server will fit best. It is also worth considering changing the web server at some point in time. It all depends on your settings. We need to realize that no matter what happens, the Zabbix frontend always needs to access the database directly.

The main configuration parameters

Here, we will try to talk about the main configuration parameters for frontend performance used by Zabbix. When considering basic items to ensure acceptable performance from the implementation of Zabbix, we basically have to activate the compression modules (mod_compress, mod_gzip, mod_deflate, and so on) in those web servers in this chapter.

Compression in Apache

For Apache, it is important to ensure that we are with the active compression module. Therefore, we must verify that mod_deflate and/or mod_gzip are installed and configured.

In httpd.conf (the location will vary according to your operational system), perform these steps:

- Check whether the module is active:

  ```
  [root]# grep deflate_module /etc/httpd/conf/httpd.conf
  LoadModule deflate_module modules/mod_deflate.so
  ```

- Add it to Zabbix's virtual host:

  ```
  <IfModule mod_deflate.c>
    AddOutputFilterByType DEFLATE text/plain
    AddOutputFilterByType DEFLATE text/css
    AddOutputFilterByType DEFLATE application/
      x-javascript AddOutputFilterByType DEFLATE text/xml
    AddOutputFilterByType DEFLATE application/xml
      AddOutputFilterByType DEFLATE application/xml+rss
      AddOutputFilterByType DEFLATE text/javascript

    # Don't compress images
    SetEnvIfNoCase Request_URI .(?:gif|jpe?g|png)$ no-gzip
      dont-vary
  </IfModule>
  ```

Basically, we are telling Apache that if mod_deflate is active, compact the types of files in AddOutputFilterByType and don't compress the images that are usually compressed.

Compression in lighttpd

In lighttpd, there is a feature ensuring module compression does not compact native dynamic content (PHP files, for example, will not be compressed). It is then necessary to enable compression of PHP itself.

Another important point is related to the fact that `mod_compress` creates a cache with the compressed files to accelerate the next request (remember that the dynamic content is not compressed by `mod_compress`). This is what we should check:

In `lighttpd.conf`, or in `modules.conf` (the location will vary according to your operating system), perform the following steps:

- Verify that the module is active:

```
server.modules = (
  ...
  "mod_compress",
  ...
)
```

- Adjust the module configuration:

```
[root]# grep ^compress /etc/lighttpd/lighttpd.conf
compress.cache-dir = "/tmp/cache/lighttpd/compress/"
compress.filetype  = ("application/x-javascript", "text/css",
"text/html", "text/plain", "text/xml", "text/javascript")
```

In `php.ini` (the location will vary according to your operational system), use the following command:

```
[root]# grep "zlib.output_compression" /etc/php.ini
...
zlib.output_compression = On
...
```

Compression in Nginx

In Nginx, using `nginx.conf` (the location will vary according to your operational system), execute the following command:

```
[root]# grep gzip /etc/nginx/nginx.conf
    gzip  on;
    gzip_comp_level 4;
    gzip_proxied any;
    gzip_types text/plain text/css application/x-javascript text/xml
application/xml application/xml+rss text/javascript;
```

Testing compression

After the changes, restart the web server (Apache, Nginx, or lighttpd) and check the logs for errors.

In a basic test with compression modules, we're able to identify that we have a considerable gain in file size. The following table shows the level of compression and page load times (`tr_staus.php` is the page that shows the status of the triggers) on a virtual server with 500 active triggers:

Compression modules	Apache without mod_deflate	Nginx without gzip	lighttpd without mod_compress	Apache with mod_deflate	Nginx with gzip	lighttpd with mod_compress
Size	1.2 MB	1.2 MB	1.2 MB	51.5 KB	51.5 KB	51.5 KB
Time	~5 sec	~6 sec	~6 sec	~5 sec	~3 sec	~4 sec

Of course, the tests may have different results with different hardware. The focus is on exemplifying how compression impacts the visualization of Zabbix screens.

If you don't have access to the web server settings (to enable the modules), you can add a small piece of PHP code in each `.php` file in Zabbix, and force compression of such files. Particularly, this alternative seems feasible only in extreme cases and when you cannot use the preceding tips.

The following code can be added to the first line of PHPs in Zabbix to perform compression:

```
ob_start("ob_gzhandler");
```

Other alternatives

There are other ways of helping the web server deliver its content faster and faster. It is common to use PHP accelerators for this task. We have some other accelerators that can be evaluated and tested in our environment:

- **Alternative PHP cache (APC)**: This is totally free and open source. It will be included in the core of PHP6. It has a rich statistics page that allows evaluation of its behavior. You can learn more about it at `http://pecl.php.net/package/APC`.

- **XCache**: This was developed by one of the creators of lighttpd. It has a very simple statistics page. A detailed information about this can be found at `http://xcache.lighttpd.net/`.

- **eAccelerator**: This was created in 2004 as a fork of Turck MMCache. It is supported by the most recent versions of PHP. To learn more about it go to `http://eaccelerator.net/`.

In practice, a PHP accelerator's main function is to improve performance of PHP scripts by caching these compiled scripts so that almost all the overhead of compiling is eliminated. PHP accelerators decrease server load and increase the speed of PHP.

The main advantage of a PHP accelerator is that scripts are compiled and loaded in the memory and then delivered to the user. With this, the amount of I/O performed on the disk is reduced. Since the memory latency is smaller than the drive's latency, we have a significant gain in user perception.

The following table shows the results of a simple test (with Apache) performed on a virtual machine by accessing the triggers screen (`tr_status.php`) with about 700 active triggers:

Test	XCache without mod_deflate	APC without mod_deflate	PHP without mod_deflate	XCache with mod_deflate	APC with mod_deflate	PHP with mod_deflate
Concurrency level	50	50	50	50	50	50
Complete requests	500	500	500	500	500	500
Document length (bytes)	24,317	24,317	24,317	24,317	24,317	24,317
Total bytes transferred	12,593,511	12,274,254	12,274,377	12,285,937	12,285,862	12,285,850

Test	XCache without mod_deflate	APC without mod_deflate	PHP without mod_deflate	XCache with mod_deflate	APC with mod_deflate	PHP with mod_deflate
Requests per second	33.39	31.28	13.50	44.05	32.01	14.72
Transfer rate (kilobytes per second)	805.12	749.86	332.66	1,058.83	774.82	353.13
Time taken	~15 sec	~16sec	~36sec	~11sec	~15sec	~34sec

As we can see, we have a considerable gain when using PHP accelerators compared to pure PHP (no use of accelerators). On the other hand, mod_deflate did not represent a very large difference in the tests.

It is also clear that XCache has performed better in the test than APC.

The suggestion is that you run the same tests in your environment so that you can find the best solution and configuration for your scenario.

For reference, tests were performed with the **Apache Bench (AB)** tool, with the following parameters:

```
[root]# ab -c 50 -n 500 -k -H "Accept-Encoding: gzip, deflate"
"http://<zabbix_gui_IP>/zabbix/tr_status.php?groupid=0&hostid=0"
```

Another alternative is the Google Pagespeed module (https://developers. google.com/speed/pagespeed/module). This module's main function is to optimize the content delivered by the web server (including CSS, JavaScript, images, and so on).

Summary

In this chapter, we provided information on how to speed up the delivery of Zabbix data to users and improve their experience with the frontend.

I would say that we should start any project using Zabbix settings `deflate/ compress/gzip` and PHP accelerators (XCache, APC, and so on) because in this way, we ensure that users have a positive experience upon their first contact with Zabbix. This is one thing we shouldn't ignore in our planning and installation of the Zabbix environment. We also know that nowadays we can choose from among the new web servers. Apache is not the sole alternative, nor is it the killer one. You will need to start your own tests and obtain your own answer for your environment.

In the next chapter, we'll talk about storage and what we need to keep in mind before (sometimes after) we start a Zabbix deployment.

6
Adjusting the Storage

All data gathered and evaluated by the triggers won't be discarded now, and will be stored for future reference, for other triggers, or to be used only for graphics, mails, and screens. The storage is where all of this data will flow to—not only item's data but also triggers and events. Now, this is a very important point to be considered: how long will we be keeping this data stored? And how does our storage behave with this mass of data, new writings, environmental growth, and consultations that will be made from this data?

In this chapter, we are going to cover these topics:

- Choosing between shared and local storage
- Configuring the storage for performance
- Small, medium, or large environments?
- What do I need for my environment?

Choosing between shared and local storage

First, I will ask a question: what is the best storage for Zabbix? This question is generic and, no doubt, the answer to it is: the fastest possible. But what is the best storage for Zabbix considering your environment? Here, the answers are many and everyone has to find their own. But why not simply use the fastest existing storage in the world? If you have that kind of cash to invest in it, it will be great for you. Zabbix will run perfectly, without performance issues and for a long time.

We have to consider that the vast majority of users and companies that make the choice of Zabbix are also in search of reduction and/or adjustments in operating costs. It makes little sense to propose a project that always considers the most modern hardware and existing edge in the market. Certainly, we need to make some settings to suit all the premises of a Zabbix deployment project. We can't forget that at the beginning of the project, we will have to make acquisitions (services, hardware, training, and so on). In some companies, it is common to reuse existing hardware for a project involving Zabbix.

In this scenario, where resources are limited, we must think about what the best storage and configuration that can be used is. We can't forget that one of the goals of this book is to understand the Zabbix data flow for better use of the hardware resources we have.

One of the recurring questions we have in forums about Zabbix, and even from customers during the project is: can I use Zabbix in a virtualized environment? As always, we have some answers to this question, and all of them take into account a number of factors that must be evaluated when making decisions.

The main point to be considered in this question is: do we intend to virtualize all the major components of Zabbix? (the database, Zabbix server, and Zabbix GUI).

Some Zabbix components can be virtualized without major concerns:

- The Zabbix server, for example, uses very little storage (more memory and CPU)
- The Zabbix GUI can also be virtualized without risking performance, considering the storage (since you can use an area in the memory for the frontend files)
- The Zabbix proxy can also be virtualized without performance issues

What about the database? Here, the scenario changes completely because the database is where all of the data will flow. Any oscillation in the storage's virtualized environment can affect the writing or reading of Zabbix and infringe the platform's performance as a whole because the Zabbix server will have difficulty delivering the data to the database (directly affecting the cache, buffer, DBSyncer, and so on), and the Zabbix GUI will have difficulties reading the data (directly affecting the graphics display, screen, maps, triggers, and so on). Especially, almost every virtualized environment will use network storage, such as the EBS in AWS. This kind of network storage will have a great impact on the IO performance, and furthermore, it will delay the data flow.

As we can see, the first point raised was to use or not to use all the virtualized Zabbix components, and this is extremely important because we need to decide between the flexibility of a virtualized environment and — as a result — a shared environment or to have the stability of a physical environment, and thereby, isolated. **Primer monitoring** teaches us that we should keep the monitoring environment as isolated as possible from our production environment (that is, the monitored environment), as an oscillation in the production environment could affect the monitoring environment. Then we may have false positives or false negatives. Other than isolation, we must carry out the monitoring of the monitoring system itself.

Some people have certainly thought that the hardware, software, and atmosphere used for virtualization today are fairly robust and meet far more critical applications and services than Zabbix, and that would be enough to decide on using a virtualized environment. But we should not blindly trust such information. For example, I have seen Zabbix suffering in times of high occupancy of shared storage cache. The bottleneck of Zabbix is always the I/O bottleneck of database hardware (physical, virtual, shared storage, and so on).

The trick is to use local storage (dedicated) whenever possible because this decision will facilitate troubleshooting when necessary. It will also allow us to isolate the monitoring environment from the production environment.

In this dedicated storage, which is the proper hardware? Does it need to be a specific hardware for storage? Can I use the local disk? What RAID should I use?

Well, here the questions become more specific and it is easier to find the answers. Even though the focus here is on performance, we can't help but think about the redundancy of such data. So, to get the answers to these questions, let's consider the alternatives to ensure performance and data security.

Do we need specific hardware for storage? I would say *no* in most environments. Usually, the disks existing on the servers are sufficient to guarantee the good performance of Zabbix. Of course, we can't fail to consider the estimated size of the database, and thus measure the size needed for the disks we intend to use. In the Zabbix manual (considering version 2.4) there is a formula that helps us understand the growth of Zabbix's database.

In reality, the size of the database should be calculated for the sizes of the tables according to these rules:

Tables	Considerations for calculating disk space
Configuration	Oscillates very little (when new hosts, items, triggers, and so on, are created in Zabbix). It is about 10 MB in size.
History	These are the largest tables in the Zabbix database. The formula for calculating the size is *days * (items / refresh rate) * 24 * 3600 * bytes*. Here, the meanings of the words are as follows: • **Days**: This denotes the number of days chosen to keep the history of the collected data • **Items**: This denotes the number of items • **Refresh rate**: This is the average time for collecting items • **Bytes**: This denotes the space required for storing each item (depending on the database engine; on average, this is 50 bytes)
Trends	Every hour, Zabbix consolidates data from the previous hour and stores this data in the Trends tables. The formula for calculating the size is *days * (items / 3600) * 24 * 3600 * bytes*. Here, the meanings of the words are as follows: • **Days**: This is the number of days for which we will keep the trends data • **Items**: This is the number of items • **Bytes**: This denotes the space required to store the trend of each item (depending on the database engine; on average, this is 128 bytes)

Tables	Considerations for calculating disk space
Events	These are tables that store the event data generated by triggers. They are not related to the tables of history and trends.
	The formula to calculate the size is *Days * Events * 3600 * 24 * bytes*.
	Here, the meanings of the words are as follows:
	• **Days**: This denotes the number of days that we store the data of events
	• **Events**: This denotes the number of events per second (in the worst case scenario, this value will be 1)
	• **Bytes**: This denotes the space required to store each event (depending on the database engine; on average, this is 130 bytes)

Considering this information, add these values: *configuration + history + trends + events*.

Thus, we obtain the total space that will be occupied by Zabbix.

It is important to emphasize and draw attention to the fact that the `events` tables can grow quite large in the case of environments with a lot of oscillations and flap triggers.

In certain environments, the `events` table can be as large as the `history` tables. This also depends on the housekeeping settings for the events (retention time).

Configuring the storage for performance

Now we need to evaluate two points: the writing speed and reading speed necessary to maintain the environment with adequate performance.

To understand and get to an estimate of the writing ability, we can use a very simple formula: *vps * bytes (new values per second * 50)*. This is considering only the entry of new values of items at the base, and not other Zabbix functions (trends, events, and so on).

For readability, we need to consider the number of users, screens, maps, quantities of items (the generation of the trends depends on the selections in the history of the tables), and so on.

With estimates of reading and writing skills being necessary for our Zabbix environment, we can choose between existing technologies and models in the market drives. There is a report (2014) that contains a comparison with some disk model brands (SATA, SAS, SSD, and so on):

Year in Review 2014 - Summary Performance Comparison by Storage Class											
Storage Class			IOPS FOB PTS WSAT - T4Q32	IOPS Steady State PTS IOPS - T2Q16 / T4Q32			Bandwidth PTS Throughput - T1Q32		Response Time PTS Latency - T1Q1	
Category	Device Type	Capacity	RND 4KiB 100% W	RND 4KiB 100% W	RND 4KiB 65:35 RW	RND 4KiB 100% R	SEQ 1024KiB 100% W	SEQ 1024KiB 100% R	RND 4KiB 100% W Ave	RND 4KiB 100% W Max
HDD & SSHD										
1	SSHD	7,200 RPM 2.5" SATA Hybrid	500 GB	134	134	131	148	107 MB/s	103 MB/s	18.54 mSec	40.63 mSec
2	SAS HDD	15,000 RPM 3.5" SAS HDD	80 GB	350	340	398	401	84 MB/s	90 MB/s	55.39 mSec	97.28 mSec
CLIENT SSDs										
3	mSATA	mSATA 1.8" MLC	128 GB	45,743	1,359	1,926	36,517	187 MB/s	533 MB/s	0.74 mSec	543.41 mSec
4	M.2 x2	M.2 x2 2280 MLC	512 GB	61,506	4,185	9,532	71,282	455 MB/s	535 MB/s	0.29 mSec	24.99 mSec
5	SATA Client	SATA8l 2.5" MLC	200 GB	54,788	33,583	50,708	63,640	367 MB/s	480 MB/s	0.06 mSec	11.95 mSec
ENTERPRISE SSDs										
6	SATA 6Gb/s	SATA 6Gb/s 2.5" eMLC	800 GB	57,422	39,561	46,072	70,604	454 MB/s	504 MB/s	0.05 mSec	0.22 mSec
7	SAS 12Gb/s	SAS 12Gb/s 2.5" MLC	800 GB	97,950	41,516	72,342	145,407	448 MB/s	973 MB/s	0.05 mSec	11.84 mSec
8	SFF 8639	SFF 8639 4 lane 2.5" MLC	700 GB	149,512	44,872	166,002	397,564	564 MB/s	1,698 MB/s	0.01 mSec	0.38 mSec
9	PCIe 8 Lane	PCIe 8 Lane Edge Card MLC	1400 GB	159,926	87,419	236,227	742,674	614 MB/s	2,673 MB/s	0.01 mSec	0.56 mSec

The source for this is http://www.storagenewsletter.com/wp-content/uploads/2015/01/Calypsossd-performance.jpg

After defining the brand model of the disks, we need to decide on whether or not a RAID is needed in our Zabbix environment. The recommendation is to use the RAID concept, as we gain performance and security.

We know that there are some RAID designs to be evaluated that can be chosen for our environment. Each model has its advantages and disadvantages. The most common is RAID10. Some environments make use of RAID5. But what is the best option for RAID anyway? Well, Zabbix SIA guides the use of RAID10 (or RAID1 + 0). The arguments for this are on the explanations of each type. There are many forums and websites talking about the advantages and disadvantages of each type of RAID. The important thing is to understand which of them is the most appropriate for Zabbix. In this case, it is correct to say that RAID5 has better read performance and RAID10 has better write performance. What about your Zabbix environment? Does it have more writings or readings, a lot of users or a few users, a lot of screens or a few screens? Again, the right choice here will depend on your environment and the hardware at hand.

It is necessary to say that RAID5 is dangerous because of the *write-hole* problem and its long rebuild time. Sometimes, we cannot endure the rebuild time because it is too long. So, RAID10 is a better choice for most environments. Another point to consider is how the RAID will behave when degraded (with one or more disk failures). In RAID5, the degraded performance is not encouraging. However, a disk failure in RAID10 has no impact on performance. What happens during the recovery of RAID? Yes, in this case, the two types are affected by environmental reconstruction tasks.

Small, medium, or large environments?

Understanding your own environment is essential for choosing the most appropriate hardware and configuration. Some users think that their environment is large when it is actually small or medium. What defines an environment as small, medium, or large? The numbers of each of these—items and vps, hosts, users, and events—are important factors in the evaluation.

If our focus here is on performance, the most important information we need is directly related to the reading and writing rates we want to achieve in our environment. According to Zabbix SIA, a very big environment is an environment that has more than 10,000 monitored hosts and a small environment has up to 20 hosts. We have a good difference between sizes, but we must remember that the amount of hosts does not *directly* reflect the number of values per second of the environment.

Consider that we have 1,000 hosts, each host has 60 items, and each item is updated every 60 seconds. So, we will have a vps of 1,000. If we had 100 hosts, each host had 600 items, and each item was updated in 60 seconds, again we would have had a vps of 1,000.

This means that the number of hosts alone does not define the environment size.

From experience within the projects in which we participate, we understand that environments can be classified according to other factors, such as these:

- **Average (or maximum) number of online users in the Zabbix GUI:** These users are most likely accessing the data on the Zabbix database and competing with the internal processes.

- **Average number of events generated in the environment per second:** This seems irrelevant, but in reality, it becomes a headache if not controlled and considered. We should remember that events are available for users who are online.

- **VPS**: No doubt, this is the main Zabbix indicator for determining the environment size. A superficial analysis might just be the only indicator for this assessment.

- **Average length of retention of items, trends, and events**: This will set the amount of data that online users can access via the GUI. It will directly impact the housekeeping tasks.

Based on this information, it is clear that we can't rely on a single metric to set the environment size and, based on that, set the appropriate hardware to guarantee the performance of Zabbix.

What do I need for my environment?

The following table helps us get a route to measure the Zabbix environment:

Size	Small	Medium	Large	Very large
Concurrent users	Less than 5	Less than 20	Less than 50	More than 50
Average number of events	Less than 1 per second	Less than 2 per second	Less than 5 per second	More than 5 per second
VPS	Less than 200	Less than 500	Less than 1000	More than 1000
Average history retention time	Less than 10 days	Less than 30 days	Less than 90 days	More than 90 days
Average trend retention time	Less than 90 days	Less than 180 days	Less than 360 days	More than 360 days

The preceding table is a reference, not an absolute rule matrix, for setting the environment size. It can be helpful to measure the hardware type and the type of storage required for each scenario. Its use is simple: consider your environment (current or future) and check how the criteria are distributed in the Small or Very large columns. The combination of these criteria is what will set the environment size to that of Zabbix.

The following table represents the environmental data with the estimated hardware and storage necessary to ensure the best performance:

Size	Small	Medium	Large	Very large
Storage type	Local desktop disks (HD)	Local enterprise disks (HD)	Local disks with RAID10 (HD)	SSD disks or fast shared storage
CPU type	Two-core CPU	Four-core CPU	16-core CPU	24-core CPU
Memory	4 GB RAM	16 GB RAM	24 GB RAM	64 GB RAM

Always remember that this information is not absolute and we can use the data from projects in which we've participated over the years to design it. It is also important to remember that while this book was being written, the Zabbix production version was 2.4 and it is with respect to the resources and capacity of this version that the estimates were made.

Summary

In this chapter, you learned what we must take into account when we think of the hardware, especially the storage, to use with Zabbix. A good discussion of RAID types can be initiated and can guarantee many hours of arguments from all sides. But without a doubt, a large environment needs to list a kind of RAID (Zabbix SIA indicates RAID10) to ensure high performance. High-performance shared storage should also be considered if the environment is actually quite large.

You also realized that you can't consider only the amount of hosts or only the vps to classify the size of the environment and then set the hardware to suit it.

Don't forget this; to get the best performance from Zabbix, we need to understand how the information is flowing into it, and adjust the settings to control the flow of data (reading and writing).

An environment that is not measured can't be controlled. The secret of Zabbix performance is directly connected to the control of the flow. In the next chapter, we'll talk about operating systems and how to adjust some small, but important, parameters that matter a lot when it comes to performance.

7

Tuning the Operating System

In the projects that I have participated to date, and even the forums that I have supported, it became apparent that users do not have any major concerns regarding the necessary adjustments to the operating system when Zabbix is run in the environment.

What happens is that every operating system has its own configuration requirements for ensuring good performance in the applications it will support. The operating system is an extremely important part of environmental deployment of Zabbix. The Zabbix SIA guides users to use the operating system with which they have more experience. And why? So that they can make the necessary adjustments to get the best performance.

And we know, in fact, what the OS performance adjustments required to support Zabbix are.

In this chapter, we will talk about these topics:

- Linux distributions and Zabbix
- The necessary adjustments in the kernel

Linux distributions and Zabbix

What happens with Zabbix also happens with almost all applications that users need and put into production—lack of planning.

Zabbix is a platform that basically consists of three components: the Zabbix server, the Zabbix database, and the Zabbix GUI. Well, each of these components has a distinct behavior and specific hardware requirements.

The database, for example, requires more IO than the Zabbix server or the Zabbix GUI. At this point, we begin to think that the kernel parameters need to be adjusted, with the aim of increasing the IO performance.

Each Linux distribution has its default features and settings. In practice, any modern Linux distribution can be used with Zabbix without any restrictions or special care, but most of them will require adjustments.

Well, we know that Zabbix can be an environmental bottleneck if our settings are not as per the hardware. The database also has a default setting that will ensure its operation with any hardware. Imagine that the database has a standard configuration of a 4 GB or 8 GB buffer, and only 2 GB RAM of hardware memory. Certainly, unpleasant things would occur. With the operating system also, it's the same; the settings and limits need to be adjusted to work in conjunction with the hardware we are using and the application that will run on this operating system.

The operating system settings can also be a bottleneck for Zabbix. Linux distributions are available with generic settings that will work reasonably well for most users and applications. In our case, we need to prepare the operating system to allow Zabbix to do its job, and it requires adjustments on details that are not aligned with certain needs.

I think the most relevant point here is understanding that we are still talking about flow control. In other words, each component involved in the collection, evaluation, storage, and display of Zabbix data (the Zabbix agent, Zabbix proxy, Zabbix server, Zabbix database, operating system, and storage) has ways of controlling the flow of such data and tasks, and we need to know the ways to adjust these flows so that we can guarantee the best performance for Zabbix.

The necessary adjustments in the Kernel

One point that has to be changed immediately is the limit on the number of open files because in certain critical situations, Linux servers generate an exception called `Too many open files`. This kind of problem occurs when a particular user (including root) reaches the maximum limit of the number of open files allowed by the system.

With Zabbix, it is no different and we need to pay attention to it. Each Zabbix server process (pollers, trappers, housekeeping, discovery, syncers, and so on) will request opening of files, both for writing and reading. It is worth stressing that a socket is also considered an open file. Zabbix usually opens many TCP/IP connections to perform data collection. Each connection will request opening of several files and sockets.

Here's a point to pay attention to because we have two parameters that are related, so much so that many users think they are the same. In fact, there is a difference in scope between the parameters, and it is related to the maximum number of open files.

User-level FD limits

Initially, we need to identify the existing limits applied to the process level (per user). The command used here is `ulimit ()`:

```
[root]# ulimit -Sa |grep files
open files                       (-n) 1024
```

In other words, the limit on the number of open files for proceedings in that operating system for root user is 1024. Probably, it will be the same for all system users, including the `zabbix` user.

Also, we need keep in mind that the Zabbix process will run with the user called `zabbix` or whichever user that you chose to run the Zabbix server:

```
[zabbix]$ ulimit -Sa |grep files
open files                       (-n) 1024
```

This means that each process performed by the `zabbix` user can use up to 1024 files (including sockets) simultaneously, and it will be the same for the user running MySQL and Apache.

Stay alert to observe this limit and, if necessary, make the required changes. The configuration file in this case is `/etc/security/limits.conf` and the parameter to be adjusted is `nofile`:

```
...
#          - nofile - max number of open file descriptors
...
```

Kernel-level FD limits

Kernel-level FD is the other parameter related to the limit on the number of open files. In this case, it is the kernel level; in a large environment, it is likely that the default limit is not suitable. Then we need to adjust it by editing the `/etc/sysctl.conf` file and add this line (change it if it already exists):

```
fs.file-max = 100000
```

This makes this value come into effect on the next boot. To enforce the change at runtime, we can use this command:

```
[root ]# sysctl -w fs.file.max=100000
```

The maximum number of files handled can be changed in the proc filesystem without reboot:

```
[root ]# echo "10000" > /proc/sys/fs/file-max
```

The value to be set depends on the size of your environment and can be multiplied a few times to meet the demand.

A key of the Zabbix itself can be used to check the value:

```
[root]# zabbix_get -s localhost -k kernel.maxfiles
1512039
```

Alternatively, we can directly ask the operating system:

```
[root]# sysctl fs.file-max
fs.file-max = 1512039
```

Changing swap behavior

Other values should be considered while changing the limits, such as the vm.swappiness kernel parameter, which controls the relative weight to the use of swap. Its value can range from 0 to 100.

Higher values force the use of swap and lower values avoid the use of swap. The default value is usually 60, and it should be changed to a lower value—something pretty close to 0 (which will use swap only to avoid out-of-memory errors). Some users choose to completely disable the use of swap for the underperforming account when the operating system uses this area.

Checking and changing this value is quite simple. Verify the actual value of vm.swappiness like this:

```
[root]# cat /proc/sys/vm/swappiness
60
```

Alternatively, you can use the sysctl command:

```
[root# sysctl vm.swappiness
vm.swappiness = 60
```

To change it, use the following command:

```
[root]# sysctl -w vm.swappiness=5
```

Here's a simpler way of doing the same:

```
[root]# echo 5 > /proc/sys/vm/swappiness
```

To make the change permanent, edit the `/etc/sysctl.conf` file and add/change the `swapiness` line to this:

```
. . .
vm.swappiness = 5
. . .
```

With this change, we can make the operating system explore more of the physical memory before resorting to swap.

Two other kernel parameters should be evaluated and, if necessary, changed to reduce the swap trend. These values will directly impact the I/O, which is very suitable for a Zabbix environment. These parameters are as follows:

- `vm.dirty_ratio`: This is the percentage of maximum memory that will be used to keep dirty data. Small values force more flushes with less data, and higher values force less flushes with more data.
- `vm.dirty_background_ratio`: When this percentage is exceeded, `pdflush` will start cleaning the pages from the cache.

In an environment with intensive I/O, such as the Zabbix database, we should consider a low value for `vm.dirty_background_ratio` and a higher value for `vm.dirty_ratio`. The recommended values for starting performance tests are as follows:

```
[root]# echo 5 > /proc/sys/vm/dirty_background_ratio
[root]# echo 60 > /proc/sys/vm/dirty_ratio
```

These two values can be tested to determine the most appropriate value for your environment. You may need low values for the two parameters. Everything will depend on the hardware involved (amount of RAM memory, CPU, disk, and so on).

Changing IO schedulers

Another point to be considered is the IO scheduler. This is a kernel parameter that should be changed to what fits best into the environment. In practice, with this parameter, we will define how the operating system will organize the I/O request.

The I/O scheduler has four possible values:

- **Completely fair queuing (CFQ)**: This is the standard in many Linux distributions. In this case, each thread has an allowed time for sending the I/O to the disk.
- **Deadline**: This is latency-oriented. Reading is favored over writing. It is recommended for use in environments with multiple disks.

- **NOOP**: This is the simplest of all algorithms. It exactly passes the I/O requests received to the disk in the same order. It is very good when used with SDD or virtual drives.

- **Anticipatory**: The anticipatory I/O scheduler is deprecated.

Well, the question now is: what's the best algorithm to use with Zabbix? The answer is that it depends on the hardware being used. What we should do is perform tests and get the best algorithm for our environment.

Some hardware manufacturers and software developers apparently have a consensus about which I/O scheduler to use in high-performance environments:

- **RedHat**: https://access.redhat.com/solutions/54164
- **Oracle**: http://www.oracle.com/us/technologies/linux/oracle-linux-with-flash-2004731.pdf
- **SuSe**: https://www.suse.com/documentation/sles-12/book_sle_tuning/data/cha_tuning_io_schedulers.html
- **HP**: http://h20564.www2.hp.com/hpsc/doc/public/display?docId=emr_na-c02574216&sp4ts.oid=4346563
- **IBM**: http://public.dhe.ibm.com/software/dw/linux390/perf/IOScheduler_Presentation_website.pdf

With these, the recommended algorithm for environments with databases is `deadline`, and should be preferred for most environments.

To check which algorithm is in use and change the runtime, use these commands:

```
[root]# cat /sys/block/xvda/queue/scheduler
noop anticipatory deadline [cfq]


[root]# echo deadline > /sys/block/xvdb/queue/scheduler


[root]# cat /sys/block/xvdb/queue/scheduler
noop anticipatory [deadline] cfq
```

With the preceding commands, we can visualize all the algorithms available for use. What is in use appears in brackets.

To make the change permanent, you need to change the `/boot/grub/grub.conf` file (depending on your boot loader) and add the option in the OS boot by simply adding the `kernel ... rhgb quiet elevator = deadline` parameter to the end of the booting line in the kernel.

We can also consider making some changes to the settings of read ahead. Remember that the SSD does not have much gain with a high read ahead (a default value of 256 seems appropriate), but the drives may have an improved reading performance with values greater than 256. To find and change the setting of your disks, use these commands:

```
[root ]# blockdev --report
RO    RA    SSZ   BSZ   StartSec          Size    Device
rw    256   512   4096          0    8589934592    /dev/xvda
rw    256   512   4096          0   21474836480    /dev/xvdc
rw    256   512   4096          0    1073741824    /dev/xvdb
```

```
[root]# blockdev --setra 1024 /dev/DEVICE
```

Some tools can be used to test the changes made and set the change that fits the hardware:

- `iostat`
- `hdparm`
- `Bonnie++`
- `dd`
- `iozone`
- `ioping`
- `fio`

You shouldn't forget that each environment has its own characteristics, mainly in terms of hardware differences. So, the tests are essential for ensuring the best configuration.

The network parameters

The network settings should be evaluated and adjusted, if necessary. The changes must be made in the `/etc/sysctl.conf` file. The recommended values are given in this table:

Parameter	Observations
`sysctl -w net.ipv4.tcp_max_syn_backlog=4096`	The maximum number of connections pending in SYN. Zabbix usually receives many connections during the collections. The default is 512, and the recommended value is 2048 or even 8192.
`sysctl -w net.ipv4.tcp_rmem="4096 87380 16777216"` `sysctl -w net.ipv4.tcp_wmem="4096 87380 16777216"`	Minimum, standard, and maximum for the buffer used by each TCP socket. We can increase the minimum value to something close to the standard. The Zabbix server and MySQL server will benefit from these adjustments.
`sysctl -w net.ipv4.tcp_fin_timeout=30`	The number of connections in Zabbix are very large and we don't intend to stay so long waiting for completion. The maximum Zabbix timeout is 30 seconds, and the default `tcp_fin_timeout` value is 60 seconds.
`sysctl -w net.ipv4.tcp_keepalive_time=600`	Most systems use a `keepalive` timeout of 7,200 seconds, which means that the system is notified about a dead connection after 2 hours. You will probably want this time to be shorter, such as 1 minute or so. For every operating system, the adjustment is done in a different way. As the number of connections is very large, we need to quickly release the ones that are broken.
`sysctl -w net.core.rmem_max=16777216` `sysctl -w net.core.wmem_max=16777216`	The maximum TCP send and receive window. The default values are very small, and they limit the operating system and the applications that run on it.

These are the main parameters to be evaluated and adjusted. But let me be repetitive—there are no magic numbers that are perfect for all environments. You must always remember that there are many variables to consider in each environment. Therefore, we should test the parameters with some values to find what is right for each environment.

Summary

The operating system is an important part of the control flow process. Be sure to have a look at your Linux distribution and the best practices for better performance. Always take into account the component that the operating system is involved with (Zabbix proxy, Zabbix GUI, Zabbix server, or Zabbix database). Each Zabbix component will need specific settings in the kernel parameters.

In the next chapter, we will discuss the steps to be taken after all the points so far have been considered in detail and evaluated and adjusted in your environment. If we still have performance problems, how can we move ahead? It is in pursuit of this response that we will go to the next chapter.

8
Doing the Extra Work

So far, we have considered and talked about Zabbix running with all of its components (the Zabbix server, Zabbix GUI, and Zabbix database) in the same hardware. With all that we have seen in the previous chapters, we have managed to achieve very good performance levels and ensure monitoring of hundreds of devices with tens of thousands of items.

However, hardware is always a limitation on Zabbix. Sometimes, we don't have the authorization or money required to purchase more powerful hardware to deal with the increase in the number of hosts and monitored items. Also, thinking about growing by increasing the hardware isn't the best option.

Each major component of Zabbix (the server, GUI, and database) requires certain portions of the overall hardware. To avoid competition, they can be divided into distinct hardware components. Thereby, we can configure the operating system to perform more specific and not so generic tasks.

In this chapter, we talk about these topics:

- Dividing the components
- Specifying the hardware for each component
- Partitioning tables

Dividing the components

Where we stand, we already understand the main adjustments required to ensure the best performance of Zabbix, but what should we do when all the suggested adjustments were made and performance is still a topic that causes headaches?

Luckily, Zabbix SIA envisaged Zabbix as a platform, and they allow us to target this platform and choose better hardware and OS configuration for each component. But when exactly is the time to think about having more than one piece of hardware to meet the demands of the environment? Is it when users complain that the GUI is slow? Is it when we have too many rows in the Zabbix server? Is it when I have too much IOWAIT in the operating system? Is it when the housekeeper takes a long time to run? Or when the database reaches a certain size? All of these? Any of these? Questions, questions and more questions!

In practice, a Zabbix environment can be born segmented if the environment's size can be planned from the beginning, but this is not always how it happens. Let's not forget that the environment we've been talking about since the beginning of this book is one that is born unpretentiously and acquires importance as it assists support teams or even the managers and directors.

In this precise scenario, you may wonder: do I need to set up a new segmented environment? Can I start from the current environment and separate only one component (the Zabbix server, GUI, or database) for some other hardware? Keep calm! Since the environment is running on a single item of hardware, it is simple enough to complete the transition. What we need to understand is which component to separate and what hardware to use.

There is no doubt that the component that requires more hardware is the Zabbix database, be it with MySQL, PostgreSQL, Oracle, or DB2. With this information, we know where the first signs that the current hardware needs support to perform the tasks required by Zabbix are. Of course, we always have some addition of alternative hardware resources (especially memory), but when that runs out, we have no choice but to opt for new hardware to support our Zabbix environment. This new hardware needs to have a very fast CPU and disks (RAID10, SSD, and so on).

Another recurring question and source of confusion is about the Zabbix server. Some users think that this is the component that requires more hardware, and tend to allocate more powerful hardware to it instead of the database. The Zabbix server will hardly be a motivator for new hardware, but we can't ignore the fact that Zabbix's caches and buffers need RAM to support the data flow control. So, a point to consider is the amount of memory allocated to the Zabbix server. The Zabbix server CPU is also something to consider, but hardly enough to deserve dedicated hardware. What about the disks? Well, the Zabbix server doesn't require much disks, so there is no need to think of a RAID10 or an SSD for this component.

What about the Zabbix GUI? Will it require new hardware just for itself? This depends on the number of online users and the number of screens, slides, maps, and graphics available in the environment. But yes, the Zabbix GUI can be one of the components that require separate hardware.

It is also important to properly understand the web server used (Apache, Nginx, lighttpd, and so on) and the alternative performance configurations. Each web server has its own characteristics and hardware requirements. Apache, for example, is the web server that has the highest memory use, so the Zabbix GUI with Apache and the Zabbix database are direct competitors in this regard.

Specifying the hardware for each component

Once we have an understanding of the need to separate the different Zabbix components in different hardware, we need to list what specifications are needed for each piece of hardware.

To make this decision, we must know the behavior of each component. Consider the following:

- Zabbix server
    - This basically receives all of the environment data and forwards it to the Zabbix database.
    - It doesn't supply the data immediately. It keeps it in the **Caches history** and delivers it later with **DBSyncers**.
    - This has large amount of network connections because of the data gathering.
    - It performs many mathematical calculations involving, mainly, triggers.
    - It has very low disk usage.

- Zabbix GUI
    - This basically displays, the data in the Zabbix database to users
    - It has reasonable disk usage (this can still keep the GUI files in a memory area)

- Zabbix database
    - This basically receives data from the Zabbix server
    - It delivers data to the Zabbix GUI
    - It needs a lot of memory to cache/buffer stock
    - It requires a multicore CPU (the more the better)
    - It has intensive disk usage (reading and writing)

With this basic list of tasks and behaviors of each component, we can start our review and determine the settings for the hardware that we will use for each task.

Since Zabbix version 1.8, we are getting more and more functions related to cache and data buffering, and it is clear that this will require more memory in the hardware in which we have the Zabbix server installed.

This table will help you understand the maximum amount of memory that we can allocate to the Zabbix cache/buffer:

Parameter	Observations
VMwareCacheSize	This stores VMware monitoring data.
	It can reach 2 GB. The default value is 8 MB and it can be monitored with these keys:
	• zabbix[vmware,buffer,used]
	• zabbix[vmware,buffer,total]
CacheSize	This stores all of the configuration data (hosts, triggers, items, and so on).
	The Zabbix server will die if this cache is full because there will be no more space to add new values.
	It can reach 8 GB. The default value is 8 MB and it can be monitored with the following keys:
	• zabbix[rcache,buffer,used]
	• zabbix[rcache,buffer,total]
HistoryCacheSize	This stores the data received from the environment (numerical data).
	When this cache is full, Zabbix stops receiving newly collected data (the queue grows in this case).
	It can reach 2 GB. The default value is 8 MB and it can be monitored using these keys:
	• zabbix[wcache,history,used]
	• zabbix[wcache,history,total]

Parameter	Observations
HistoryTextCacheSize	This stores the data received from the environment (text/char).
	When this cache is full, Zabbix stops receiving newly collected data (the queue grows in this case).
	It can reach 2 GB. The default value is 16 MB and it can be monitored with these keys:
	• zabbix[wcache,text,used]
	• zabbix[wcache,text,total]
TrendCacheSize	This stores the trend data before sending it to the database.
	When this cache is full, Zabbix waits for the release of space to continue with the data consolidation tasks.
	It can reach 2 GB. The default value is 4 MB and it can be monitored with the following keys:
	• zabbix[wcache,trend,used]
	• zabbix[wcache,trend,total]
ValueCacheSize	This stores information about macros and items (for use in functions and calculations without accessing the database).
	When this cache is full, Zabbix enters low-memory mode, when it can't receive more data but is still available for reading.
	It can reach 64 GB. The default value is 8 MB and can be monitored with these keys:
	• zabbix[vcache,buffer,used]
	• zabbix[vcache,buffer,total]

As we can see, the Zabbix server can require quite a large amount of RAM. The trick is to start with low values (4 GB) and increase as the requirement grows. Caches that I like to keep high (preferably with the maximum value) are HistoryCacheSize and HistoryTextCacheSize. This is because they are the "safe areas" where the Zabbix server stores data to be delivered to the database. In other words, it is the time when we run out of space for recording data in the database or the times when the storage/bank is slower to write to.

Other than this, we have the memory footprint of internal processes (pollers, syncers, trappers, and so on). They do not require much memory but can't be disregarded.

It is important to emphasize that Zabbix's process of data collection does not depend on the database, and (to some extent) it is possible for pollers and trappers to continue to receive environmental data and put in **History** caches until they are completely full. Similarly, pollers and trappers continue reading configuration data directly from the **Config** cache.

The following diagram helps us understand the relationships of caches and buffers with the internal processes of Zabbix, and how memory consumption can be high for the Zabbix server:

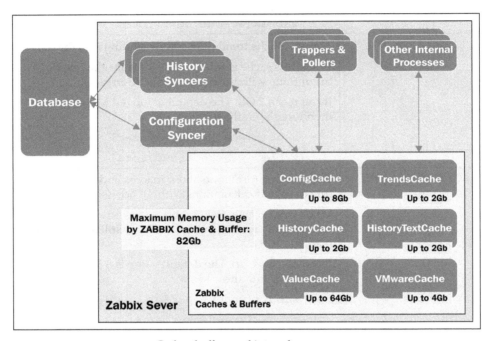

Caches, buffers, and internal processes

The CPU is also very important for the Zabbix server because it is the CPU that will run all the mathematical calculations for the functions, triggers, calculated items and aggregates. The trick is to use—undoubtedly—a good multicore CPU.

With the Zabbix GUI, things are not very different. We need to know how much memory each thread or connected user may require from the hardware. It also depends on the web server being used. However, we don't have a very strong requirement of hardware for the Zabbix GUI. In most situations, a fast multicore CPU and 4 GB (8 GB if there are many screens, maps, graphs, and so on) of RAM will suit the environment without any problems.

We can also think of keeping the Zabbix GUI in a virtualized environment, or more than one piece of hardware attending this service (DNS round-robin or a hardware/software balancer).

An important point to pay attention to is that the Zabbix API accesses Zabbix data through its PHP gateway. When there is a high pressure from invoking Zabbix API, such as data ETL, the box where the Zabbix GUI is running will take the most amount of pressure. When we need to optimize the performance of the Zabbix GUI, we can use a load balancer, such as Nginx, and put several PHP servers behind it.

What about the Zabbix database? Well, here the hardware necessary to ensure good performance in a large environment can be really high. We must remember that when we reach the point of targeting components and different hardware, we have already made every suggested adjustment possible to maintain the environment within a single piece of hardware. Moreover, the Zabbix database is the component that will require segmentation because it needs to consume more hardware resources than the other two components. So, it is natural that this is the biggest hardware component.

And what should the hardware be? We should start by considering a 16 or 24 core CPU. The Zabbix database will really demand a lot of CPU resources, and so we can't neglect this item. Memory will also be of utmost importance to ensure good environmental performance of the Zabbix database. We must remember that for MySQL, it is recommended to have 80 percent of the memory dedicated to `BufferPoolSize`, which is the bank's portion that we will handle in the memory. With this in mind, our Zabbix database must begin with something between 16 GB and 32 GB of memory, and it may require 64 GB or more, depending on the environment size.

With this segmentation and the appropriate hardware for each component, we will achieve a few thousand vps without hassle.

Partitioning tables

A common practice in previous versions of Zabbix (1.4, 1.6, and even 1.8) was partitioning of database tables. This trick was used mainly as an alternative to disabling the housekeeper in critical situations for storage.

The housekeeper has the task of cleaning the database, and this cleaning is very important and necessary for Zabbix, otherwise the database will grow and exhaust the available space. Also there is data that, while not being a problem for the space, is no longer needed and we do not want to keep it in the database.

This task first involves finding out which records need to be eliminated. To do this, the housekeeper need to make a lot of SELECT statements to discover old trends, history, items not belonging to any host, events, and the session's audit log. After identifying the records that need to be eliminated, the housekeeper runs the DELETE statements.

All of these steps result in competition in reading and writing to the database, and this competition may affect performance in environments that are already close to the limit. So, we may need to disable the housekeeper, and with it disabled, we'll need another solution to clean up the old data. The alternative is to partition the database tables each month. In other words, we would have the table of history (and others) with files separated by date. Then, the cleaning would be done with a simple rm command, without any competition in the database.

Well, this practice has fallen into disuse, primarily by cache and buffer resources that Zabbix has received with each new version. With the increase of these resources, Zabbix has needed lesser direct access to the database. Basically, Zabbix SIA has segmented internal processes into backend processes and frontend processes. The frontend processes meet the demands that can't wait for a recording time (pollers, trappers, and so on). The backend processes are precisely what write these records in the background (DBSyncers, housekeeper, and so on).

From my experience and understanding of Zabbix, I don't see a need for partitioning tables, mainly because this change makes the Zabbix environment require special care. In the current version of Zabbix (2.4), automatic migration of a database can generate some headache with partitioned tables.

It is also worth remembering that since version 2.2 of Zabbix, we can control the behavior of housekeeping with more granularity and detail. This allows us to reduce the impact of this process on the database. The following screenshot shows the possibilities for adjustments to housekeeping:

Housekeeping configuration options

I understand that if all the adjustments are made correctly in certain components, we will not need partitioning of Zabbix database tables. Yet, it is a viable alternative and we can't ignore its use in extreme situations.

For those who want to know more about table partitioning, and perhaps venture into this scenario, you can visit these sites:

- `http://www.zabbix.org/wiki/Docs/howto/mysql_partition`
- `http://www.zabbix.org/wiki/Docs/howto/mysql_partitioning`
- `http://www.zabbix.org/wiki/Docs/howto/zabbix2_postgresql_partitioning`

The definition for segmentation of Zabbix's components on different pieces of hardware, for performance purposes, should be done after all the adjustments have been made to the environment.

I've had experience with customers and users who took the decision to segment in the first performance issue signals, without first assessing the variables subject to adjustments. It seems to me that a lack of understanding about the flows of Zabbix or the need for immediate change is the factor that leads to a hasty decision.

Of course, if we are already planning a large environment, it is right to think about environmental segmentation since the beginning, but it doesn't necessarily need to be born with segmented hardware. We may start with all-in-one hardware and plan to segment over time.

Summary

In this chapter, you realized that it is possible to target the components of Zabbix (the Zabbix server, GUI, and database) on different pieces of hardware. With this, we can explore the hardware and operating system settings for the best performance of each component. We also saw that there are actions that can support the performance items that are external to Zabbix (partitioning). It also became clear that the greatest hardware consumer is the Zabbix database, and it is this component that must be given the best hardware. Then we saw that the Zabbix server and GUI can coexist on the same hardware without many performance issues, while the Zabbix database acts alone on some other hardware.

In the next chapter, we will talk about the power of the Zabbix proxy and the usage of this component. We will lay emphasis on how the Zabbix proxy helps the server's performance.

Using the Zabbix Proxy

The Zabbix proxy feature appeared in version 1.6. It was meant to cater to a very specific requirement, as shown in this Zabbix SIA announcement:

```
[Zabbix-announce] ZABBIX 1.6 released
From: Alexei Vladishev <alexei.vladishev@za...> - 2008-09-18 13:47:37
...
:: ZABBIX Proxy Process

ZABBIX Proxy is a lightweight process, which collects data on behalf of
ZABBIX Server. The proxies can be used in order to centralize monitoring
of remote locations by reporting to the central server or one of ZABBIX
nodes in the distributed environment.

ZABBIX Proxy simplifies deployment and maintenances of the centralized
distributed monitoring significantly.
...
```

The Zabbix proxy was thought of so that the Zabbix server could access data on remote networks in a simpler way and without requiring to open ports or adjustments to firewall rules. The Zabbix proxy could then be placed on a remote network, access all the hosts to be monitored, and then send that data to the Zabbix server, facilitating monitoring of remote environments.

How can Zabbix proxy be a great ally in performance?

It's this that we are going to talk about in this chapter, and we will cover the following topics:

- The Zabbix proxy and the Zabbix performance
- First steps with the Zabbix proxy
- Firewall settings
- Hardware for the Zabbix proxy

The Zabbix proxy and Zabbix performance

Well, when version 1.6 was released, it gave us a new feature—a certain Zabbix proxy. The users started to explore it really soon. Those who had difficulties in monitoring remote locations before now had a smile of satisfaction and immediately installed Zabbix proxy on their environments.

Zabbix proxy didn't have an approach related to supporting Zabbix's performance. Even today, some users and training participants are surprised to realize that Zabbix proxy can be a strong performance ally.

As the main objective of Zabbix proxy was to access the remote networks that the Zabbix server couldn't reach, it was created with a single stream. Zabbix proxy was the one that opened connections with the Zabbix server, and was the one that delivered the collected connections to the Zabbix server or fetched new configuration data from it. In other words, the connections were only from the inside out—from the Zabbix proxy to the Zabbix server.

Zabbix proxy is a remote probe and has the same data collection functions that the Zabbix server has (SNMP, agents, web monitoring, and so on). The following diagram shows the view of Zabbix SIA for Zabbix proxy:

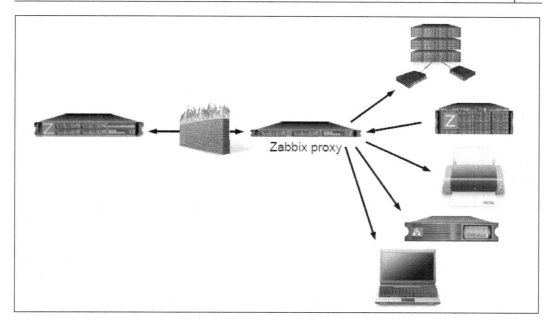

It happened that users and Zabbix SIA realized that Zabbix proxy could take data collection and management functions from the collection queue. In the early chapters of this book, we talked about *active item's use whenever possible* because we used a Zabbix proxy to make collections on behalf of the Zabbix server. Calm down! There will not be a mass update of all items and all of them will be set to **Zabbix Active**. What happens in practice is that the Zabbix proxy takes the responsibility of the hosts that have been delegated to it, and therefore the responsibility of collection of items belonging to these hosts. Thus, it collects the values of the items of the hosts and delivers them to the Zabbix server via trappers. Then, the Zabbix server does not have to worry about collecting these items.

When it became clear that the Zabbix proxy could alleviate the Zabbix server, taking over the collections that are on remote networks, it was also clear that Zabbix proxy could help the Zabbix server, even if you were on the same LAN, assuming all collections and releasing the Zabbix server for other tasks, such as evaluating triggers and functions, displaying graphics, sending alerts, and so on.

Some new approaches came into being after that point, such as more than one Zabbix proxy in the same local network as the Zabbix server. This is because the Zabbix proxy can also be overwhelmed in large environments. It could even target collections of different types in a separate Zabbix proxy (one Zabbix proxy is responsible for SNMP collections, one for collections of Windows' servers, one for Linux, one for the database, and so on). It is also worth having a Zabbix proxy per VLAN to target collections as much as possible.

Another approach that surprises some users is a Zabbix server and a Zabbix proxy in the same hardware. What would the performance gain be in this case, if the collections flow to the same hardware? Knowing the components of Zabbix well makes it easy to understand.

The Zabbix proxy works with the same databases as the Zabbix server (Oracle, MySQL, PostgreSQL, IBM DB2, and SQLite3). We may use the Zabbix proxy with one database and the Zabbix server with another database. Imagining that we want to use both on the same OS, we will choose to separate the databases, having MySQL on the Zabbix server and SQLite3 for Zabbix proxy. Here, we can set the two components on the same OS.

Another important piece of information is as follows: Zabbix proxy collects the data and delivers it to the Zabbix server. The data after being delivered is no longer needed. What if we use the SQLite3 in a memory database area? With this information, I think it is already clear what the advantage of using the Zabbix Proxy and Zabbix server on the same OS is.

In practice, we relieve the Zabbix server database and storage, as we will be performing the heavy lifting of the collections directly with Zabbix proxy, and using a part of the memory for SQLite3. This strategy is useful for easing the burden on the Zabbix server.

In fact, today Zabbix proxy plays an important role in Zabbix's performance. We must understand where and when to use this feature to support the environment. It is common to think of an environment with at least one Zabbix proxy to support the data collection, even when it is sided with the Zabbix server and on the same LAN (or the same OS).

The first steps with the Zabbix proxy

After understanding that the environment was born without a Zabbix proxy and knowing that we need to introduce this feature to the environment, what should we do? What are the precautions to take and the key areas to focus on?

Zabbix proxy is a program that must be installed in the same manner as the Zabbix server, by leaving the source, or through packages. The options in building, if not installed through packages, should be the same as those used for the Zabbix server (except that you may need to change `enable-server` to `enable-proxy`). The configuration file is almost the same as that for the Zabbix server, except the parameters related to their own settings (of Zabbix proxy). These are the parameters:

- `ProxyMode`: This parameter defines how the Zabbix proxy will behave in active mode (value 0), or in passive mode (option 1). Active mode is the standard. It was introduced in version 1.8.3. The choice of modes has little influence on performance. Instead, the idea is to try to use as many active connections as possible because in this way, we have fewer tasks performed by the Zabbix server, even in an environment with a few hundreds of Zabbix proxies. In addition to choosing the way, in this parameter, it is also necessary that the Zabbix server knows which mode the Zabbix proxy is using. This is done directly in the Zabbix GUI. Remember that the Zabbix proxy, unlike the Zabbix agent, will work only in one mode (active or passive), not both.

- `Hostname`: This parameter defines how the Zabbix proxy will present itself to the Zabbix server. This name must be the same as that created in the Zabbix GUI. Otherwise, the Zabbix proxy will not be recognized and answer the Zabbix server.

- `ProxyLocalBuffer`: This is the time in hours for which the Zabbix proxy maintains data in the local database, even after delivering it to Zabbix server. It can be 0 if we don't want to access the data on the Zabbix proxy database.

- `ProxyOfflineBuffer`: This is the time in hours for which the Zabbix proxy keeps the data in the local base until it is delivered to the Zabbix server. It must be the time (in hours) we can manage to work without the Zabbix server.

- `HeartbeatFrequency`: This is valid only for an active Zabbix proxy. It is the time in seconds for which the Zabbix proxy sends a heartbeat signal to the Zabbix server. This time is disregarded if the Zabbix proxy has to deliver data to the Zabbix server in the interval (the heartbeat has already occurred when the Zabbix proxy delivers data or searches for settings).

- `ConfigFrequency`: This is valid only for the active Zabbix proxy. It is the time in seconds at which the Zabbix proxy contacts Zabbix server to check the new settings (hosts, items, keys, and so on). The default time is 3,600 seconds, a very high time. The recommendation is something between 900 and 1,800 seconds, or any other value that is appropriate for the environment. It's important not to leave it too low, since it may impact the Zabbix server's performance, especially with a large number of Zabbix proxies.

- `DataSenderFequency`: This is valid only for the active Zabbix proxy. Here lies the main parameter of the Zabbix proxy, which is related to Zabbix's performance. This is the time in seconds in which the Zabbix proxy delivers the data collected from the environment for the Zabbix server. By default (at least until version 2.4), this time is 1 second. What if this time was 5 seconds or more? We would be creating a data buffer in the Zabbix proxy. Making fewer TCP connections to deliver this data to the Zabbix server consequently leads to less `INSERT` statements with the same amount of data. The suggestion is to consider a value somewhere between 5 and 10 seconds at the beginning, and seek adjustments if necessary. Don't forget that until this data gets to the Zabbix server, the triggers are not evaluated.

- `Server`: This is where we enter the Zabbix server's IP address or DNS name to which the proxy will report. It is important to remember that this Zabbix server will meet the demand from the Zabbix proxy with the available trappers.

- `ServerPort`: This is where we are informed that the port (`10051` by default) in the Zabbix server, set by the previous parameter, is accepting connections.

In the Zabbix server GUI and config file, there are also some parameters related to Zabbix proxies, but they are used for only those Zabbix proxies that are working in passive mode. The parameters are as follows:

- `ProxyPollers`: This is the number of pollers dedicated to contact with a passive Zabbix proxy. In theory, we should have one poller for each Zabbix proxy environment if it wants to attend all of them simultaneously, but this is not always desired. This value should be somewhere between 30 percent and 50 percent of the number of Zabbix proxy environments, so we also maintain a control flow at this point. Processing of the new data is very fast and `ProxyPollers` sits idle for a long time. In practice, suppose we have an environment with many Zabbix proxies and have some downtime on the Zabbix server. Then, when the Zabbix server gets back, all `ProxyPollers` will try to fetch the data contained in `ProxyOfflineBuffer` of each Zabbix proxy at the same time, and this can lead to an overload on the Zabbix server. So, if the data has already been collected and is secure in the Zabbix proxy, we can delay a bit the receipt of such data to ensure high performance of the Zabbix server. For this, we limit `ProxyPollers` to a number smaller than the number of passive Zabbix proxies we have in the environment.

- `ProxyConfigFrequency`: This is the frequency in seconds for which the Zabbix server pushes the new settings to the Zabbix proxy. The default is 3,600 seconds, a time too high for more dynamic environments. The trick is to use something between 600 and 1,800 seconds.

- `ProxyDataFrequency`: This is the time in seconds that the Zabbix server takes while asking Zabbix proxy for the collected data. The default is 1 second, a very short time. The recommendation is to start with 5 seconds, or even more if this delay can be accepted by the environment.

From this point, and with attention to these parameters, we can start using a Zabbix proxy. In the Zabbix GUI, using the **Host Configuration** menu or the **Management** menu, we can change the hosts that will be responsible for each Zabbix proxy created in the environment:

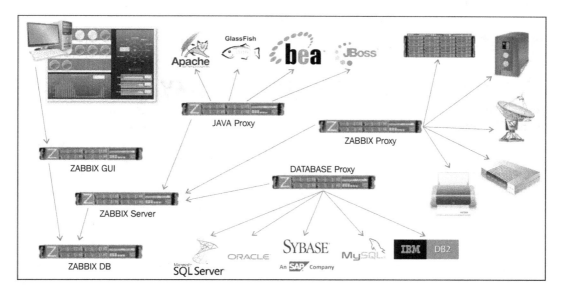

With this model in mind, it is very simple to increase the number of Zabbix proxies. The settings and adjustments in this case are minimal. So, keep in mind that it is quite a valid plan to have at least one Zabbix proxy in the same local network where we have the Zabbix server.

The firewall settings

When we begin using a Zabbix proxy in our environment, we need to take care of the data flow and the open ports or firewall rules.

In a non-Zabbix-proxy environment, it is necessary for the Zabbix server to have access to all the hosts monitored at the ports used for data collection. If we have several remote networks, we must provide the necessary firewall rules.

When we begin using a Zabbix proxy, the flow changes and the needs are much smaller. This makes it easier to negotiate with the security personnel. In this case, we only need to ensure that the Zabbix proxy and Zabbix server are able to exchange information through port `10051` TCP on both the sides.

So, the environment can now be envisioned using at least one Zabbix proxy. Always keep the rules to ensure that the Zabbix proxy and Zabbix server can establish communication through port 10051.

Some OSes will enable SELinux, which means security Linux by default. We need to disable it and remember to check the maximum open files in ulimit and the iptables settings.

Hardware for the Zabbix proxy

Some users and customers think that the Zabbix proxy requires as much hardware as the Zabbix server. This idea is wrong. The Zabbix proxy is tasked with data collection without even evaluating whether the data type is in accordance with the configuration item. In other words, the Zabbix proxy is so simple that the hardware is minimized. Zabbix SIA says that, and re-emphasizes the fact that, the Zabbix proxy can be used embedded in dedicated hardware. Some companies even sell dedicated appliances for it. What should be the size of the Zabbix proxy hardware? In practice, some rules for hardware for the Zabbix server also apply to the Zabbix proxy.

The most important information to size up the hardware for the Zabbix proxy is the vps. In modest hardware (such as Raspberry Pi model A) with a 700 MHz CPU and 256 MB of RAM, we can get more than 250 vps.

Remember that this equipment (such as the Raspberry Pi) usually makes use of an SD card or microSD card that has limited speed and life. Therefore, it is common to allocate an area in the memory to store the SQLite3 data file.

It is also important to note that there are other pieces of hardware that, just like the Raspberry Pi, have low cost and can be used to board the Zabbix proxy:

*   BeagleBone Black
*   Cubieboard
*   Banana Pi
*   Raspberry Pi
*   Hackberry A10

These and other low-cost hardware can be used smoothly for a Zabbix proxy.

Another point to note is that a Zabbix proxy can also be used in a virtual machine. Always consider the fact that oscillations in the virtualization environment can affect data gathering.

It is also worth mentioning that the load on a Zabbix proxy is so small that it can be installed on an OS that already exists in a remote network; that is, if we have any hardware running on a Linux in a remote network, we can install Zabbix proxy there without problems.

Summary

In this chapter, we understood how Zabbix proxy can be a powerful ally of the Zabbix server to improve environmental performance.

We also talked about SQLite3 being the most suitable database to use with Zabbix proxy, and saw that this choice allows us to use an area in the memory to keep this database, which is quite simple and does not require many configurations.

Another important point is the possibility of using Zabbix proxy embedded in single-board hardware. This makes deployment of this resource in a distributed environment much cheaper.

It is good practice to start the environment by considering a Zabbix proxy, even if it is on the same network where we have the Zabbix server.

Zabbix proxy lives up to its nickname: the great little helper.

In the next chapter, we will address a very important issue, which is sometimes overlooked by Zabbix administrators — the health of Zabbix. Zabbix SIA provides several item keys so that we can take care of Zabbix and monitor it just as we intend to monitor other systems, applications, and services. And we will understand the usefulness of monitoring and how we can support this data for performance tuning.

10
Monitoring the Health of Zabbix

Zabbix's internal keys have existed since version 1.6, but only in the newer versions have they gotten a wider range. Interestingly, however, Zabbix's internal keys can be termed as the "monitors that monitor other monitors". In practice, we need to measure Zabbix's behavior so that we can take decisions about what changes to make. But just knowing the internal keys of Zabbix is not enough. We need to know what each one of them means and what the effects of a change in any of the parameters related to the keys can be.

Zabbix's internal metrics are an important part of the decisions on performance tuning of an environment. This metrics can't be evaluated alone; we need to understand that they could be affected by other factors, such as the Zabbix database's settings.

The important thing here is to understand that there are no "magic settings" or "silver bullets" that can ensure best performance in any environment. Monitoring and evaluation of specific metrics for each component should always be done. Even if the environment does not present signs of trouble, we can't neglect such collections, as the assessment of historical data will be valuable. In this chapter, we are going to talk about these topics:

- Zabbix queue
- Server and proxy internal items
- Database performance items

The Zabbix queue

Ever since Zabbix was born, one of the key performance indicators has been the item's queue. If the queue is flowing and is not accumulating items, it means that Zabbix is performing well. Just like that? Almost! The queue is certainly one of Zabbix's performance indicators if our focus is only on data collection. A low queue means that Zabbix can make their collections without difficulty, but a high queue is no single indicator to pinpoint performance problems with Zabbix. However, the queue is an indicator that something is not right, which could be a problem with Zabbix, a host, a host group, or even a part of a network. A high queue will require more efforts and work from Zabbix. This high queue can be the cause of performance problems and not the consequence. It is in this view that, in my understanding, the importance of keeping the queue of Zabbix under control lies. There are specific internal items for monitoring the Zabbix queue.

One of them is `zabbix[queue,<from>,<to>]`. This, in fact, is the only internal item directly related to the Zabbix queue. It has great importance as a performance indicator. The parameters it receives are `from` and `to`, which are the delay times we need to measure the queue.

What can these parameters alone indicate? They indicate that we have a queue in some of the intervals defined by the parameters.

For example, suppose we create the following items in Zabbix:

- `zabbix[queue,1,10]`
- `zabbix[queue,11,30]`
- `zabbix[queue,31,60]`
- `zabbix[queue,61,300]`
- `zabbix[queue,301,600]`
- `zabbix[queue,600]`

In this case we will have, translated into items, the same view of the Zabbix queue screen. The intervals are the same, and we get a view of the historical values of these items.

From the creation of the items, we can create triggers to generate alerts if a queue of 10 minutes (600 seconds) exceeds 10 percent of the items. And how would this trigger be? Simple! We need an item that contains the number of active items in Zabbix, like zabbix[items]. This item will contain the total number of active items (including unsupported ones) from the environment.

The path from here to the creation of the trigger is quite simple and something familiar for most of you. We use ({Zabbix server:zabbix[queue,600].last()}/ {Zabbix server:zabbix[items].last()}=0)>0.10. In this case, we have an alert when the queue of overdue items, with more than 10 minutes, exceeds 10 percent of the total active items. Of course, this threshold should be set with different values for each environment.

And how can this trigger help with regard to performance? Well, we know that a high queue, for any reason, will directly impact the occupation of pollers, and this can end up generating those unwanted graphs with gaps.

The tip here is to create controls in the Zabbix queue so that we know when the queue exceeds a certain level. Try to keep the limit at approximately 5 percent.

An important piece of information that should be understood by Zabbix administrators is what the Zabbix queue is and what it is not. Many think that there is a table where Zabbix stores a Zabbix queue, but that's not how it works. The queue itself does not exist. What happens is that every item stores within itself (in the database and ConfigCache) some information that allows Zabbix to calculate the size of the queue. An example of the information is as follows:

- Delay: This is the time set in the item for the occurrence of each data collection. It is the frequency with which Zabbix updates the value of an item.

- LastClock: This is the timestamp of the last data collection for the item. It is the time when the Zabbix server received the last collected value for the item. With this information recorded, the Zabbix GUI can do the calculations required to display the screen of Zabbix queue. In other words, the queue does not really exist but is a calculus, considering the parameters and information about the items.

Server and proxy internal items

In addition to the Zabbix queues, the internal items allow us to identify the behavior of important points of Zabbix. But a review of the internal metrics can't be thought of alone. The value of a metric may be altered due to another metric that is not being evaluated. Correlation of metrics is something that cannot fail to occur.

In this section, we will talk about the major internal items that are directly related to Zabbix's performance. We will also explore the possible values and the likely consequences and impact of changes in these values.

This table will help you learn more about each of these metrics:

Internal key	Details
• `zabbix[items]` • `zabbix[items_unsupported]`	These two items help us keep Zabbix's unsupported items clean, which are great villains with respect to performance. The trick is to have a trigger that calculates the percentage of unsupported items and generate alerts if this value is exceeded. Usually, we work with a 2 percent limit. Thus, the trigger will be (`{Zabbix server:zabbix[items_ unsupported]. last()}/{Zabbix server:zabbix[items]. last()}=0)>0.02`.
• `zabbix[process,"history syncer",1,busy]` • `zabbix[process,"history syncer",2,busy]` • `zabbix[process,"history syncer",N,busy]`	We can see the maximum percentage of time for which each history syncer was busy during the last minute. We know (since *Chapter 3, Tuning the Zabbix Server*) that a history syncer's mission is to take data from the Zabbix cache to the Zabbix database. A high number here means that we have latency in writing to the database. It's important to remember that a history syncer also has the task of updating **Value Cache**. To know the amount of syncer's history without reading the configuration file, we can use other parameters in the same key, such as `zabbix[process,"history syncer",count]`.

Internal key	Details
• `zabbix[process,"configuration syncer",avg,busy]`	This is the synchronizer of the configuration data. Zabbix updates this cache every 60 seconds by default. Its task is to read the data from the Zabbix database and write it to the Zabbix cache. Higher numbers here mean latency in reading from the database. The result is the percentage of time for which the process was busy in the last minute. The third parameter in this key is related to the following can be: `avg`, `count`, `max`, or `min`.
• `zabbix[process,"trapper",busy]`	This parameter helps us understand how long the trappers take to receive and store data arriving from the active Zabbix proxy, the active Zabbix agent, or from the Zabbix sender. This item works only with the Zabbix cache, not with the Zabbix database. It should be constant, and an increase means that we are slow to write to the Zabbix cache.
• `zabbix[process,housekeeper,avg, busy]`	This is a very important metric. This measurement will help you understand when the housekeeper becomes one of the points of attention for Zabbix's performance. The longer the housekeeper stays busy, the more it competes with other processes. Values between 10 and 30 minutes are good. Higher values should be evaluated and treated (by setting the parameter to `MaxHousekeeperDelete` in `zabbix_server.conf`; this parameter helps only if the housekeeper has to clean a lot of the deleted item's history and trends).

Internal key	Details
• `zabbix[process,proxy poller,avg,busy]`	This parameter is concerned with the internal pollers that interact with the passive Zabbix proxy. It is important to monitor the pollers. Higher numbers indicate that we can slow down the search data in the Zabbix proxy.

The preceding keys are the most used keys for identifying points of adjustments in Zabbix. It's important to be aware that every new release of Zabbix has new keys or new parameters for existing keys.

Once again, I want to emphasize the importance of understanding exactly what each metric means and how the internal process behaves. Then, we can take more effective action because we will have properly evaluated the values received.

Take as an example the `zabbix [process, "configuration Syncer", 1, busy]` internal key. We understand that this internal process (**Configuration Syncer**) is unique and that we cannot increase the amount of concurrent processes for that function. We also know that **Configuration Syncer**, by default (`CacheUpdateFrequency` is equal to `60`), updates the configuration cache every sixty 60 seconds. Well, with this information, we understand that we cannot have the maximum occupancy of 100 percent in the last minute. This means that we are on the edge. Alternatively, we need to find a way to improve the update time of the cache or change the time to perform the update over longer intervals.

How can we improve the update time of the cache? The first thing we need to understand is what tasks **Configuration Syncer** runs. The following table shows, in summary form, the times for each type of task performed by **Configuration Syncer** in each cache update:

Item/Table	Task	Time	Task	Time
config	sql	0.000243	sync	0.000168
hosts	sql	0.008536	sync	0.001339
host_invent	sql	0.000247	sync	0.000175
templates	sql	0.000808	sync	0.000842
globmacros	sql	0.000196	sync	0.000157
hostmacros	sql	0.001796	sync	0.002339
interfaces	sql	0.000963	sync	0.001086
items	sql	0.736449	sync	0.170321

Item/Table	Task	Time	Task	Time
triggers	sql	1.393027	sync	0.028283
trigdeps	sql	0.001688	sync	0.006466
functions	sql	0.536628	sync	0.080035
expressions	sql	0.000270	sync	0.000189

The total time for the `sql` task is 2.680851 and for the `sync` task is 0.291400. This sums up the total time to 2.972251. With this information, we can see that **Configuration Syncer** spends more time collecting the data (in the database) to be taken to the cache than writing the data to the cache (in memory). So now, what can be adjusted to speed up the synchronization process of Zabbix settings? Improve the reading scores of database.

Does this assessment apply to all internal processes? Definitely not! Each internal process has its own peculiarities. To see how each internal process behaves, we can increase the debug levels individually.

For example, if we want to know what one of the internal processes of the trapper is doing, we can use the following command (available since version 2.4):

```
[root]# zabbix_server -R log_level_increase="trapper"
zabbix_server [12497]: command sent successfully


[root]# tail -f /tmp/zabbix_server.log
trapper #1 [processing data]
trapper got '...'
In recv_proxyhistory()
query [txnlev:0] [select hostid,status from hosts where host='Zabbix
Server' and status in (5,6)]
query [txnlev:0] [update hosts set lastaccess=1426959929 where
hostid=10305]
In process_hist_data()
In process_mass_data()
End of process_mass_data()
End of process_hist_data():SUCCEED
In zbx_send_response()
zbx_send_response() '{"response":"success"}'
End of zbx_send_response():SUCCEED
End of recv_proxyhistory()
trapper #1 [processed data in 0.161649 sec, waiting for connection]
```

With this, we can see exactly what internal process the trapper performs every time. This is how it works with all internal Zabbix processes. By knowing them, we can direct our actions to adjust the appropriate parameters for each type of task being performed by the internal processes.

Another example is the housekeeper. In the following code, you can see how this internal process behaves (using the `zabbix_server -R log_level_increase="housekeeper"` command):

```
[root]# tail -f /tmp/zabbix_server.log
executing housekeeper
housekeeper [connecting to the database]
housekeeper [removing old history and trends]
In housekeeping_history_and_trends() now:1431807772
End of housekeeping_history_and_trends():39339
housekeeper [removing deleted items data]
In housekeeping_cleanup()
query [txnlev:0] [select housekeeperid,tablename,field,value from
housekeeper where tablename in ('history','history_log','history_
str','history_text','history_uint','trends','trends_uint') order by
tablename]
End of housekeeping_cleanup():0
housekeeper [removing old events]
In housekeeping_process_rule() table:'events' filter:'source=0 and
now:1430751300
End of housekeeping_process_rule():0
In housekeeping_process_rule() table:'events' filter:'source=1 and
object=1' min_clock:1426964682 now:1430751300
End of housekeeping_process_rule():0
In housekeeping_process_rule() table:'events' filter:'source=1 and
object=2' min_clock:1426964682 now:1430751300
End of housekeeping_process_rule():0
In housekeeping_process_rule() table:'events' filter:'source=2 and
object=3' min_clock:1426964682 now:1430751300
End of housekeeping_process_rule():0
In housekeeping_process_rule() table:'events' filter:'source=3 and
object=0' min_clock:1426894050 now:1430751300
End of housekeeping_process_rule():0
In housekeeping_process_rule() table:'events' filter:'source=3 and
object=4' min_clock:1426894061 now:1430751300
```

```
End of housekeeping_process_rule():0

In housekeeping_process_rule() table:'events' filter:'source=3 and
object=5' min_clock:1426964682 now:1430751300

End of housekeeping_process_rule():0

housekeeper [removing old sessions]

In housekeeping_sessions() now:1430751300

End of housekeeping_sessions():0

housekeeper [removing old service alarms]

In housekeeping_process_rule() table:'service_alarms' filter:'' min_
clock:1426964682 now:1430751300

End of housekeeping_process_rule():0

 [removing old audit log items]

In housekeeping_process_rule() table:'auditlog' filter:'' min_
clock:1425934998 now:1430751300

End of housekeeping_process_rule():0

housekeeper [deleted 415355 hist/trends, 0 items, 1954 events, 25
sessions, 0 alarms, 0 audit items in 712.186100 sec, idle 1 hour(s)]
```

First, the housekeeper performs a lot of SELECT SQL statements to find the records that need to be removed from the Zabbix database. After that, it performs a lot of DELETE SQL statements to effectively remove these records from the Zabbix database. What if this process is taking too long to run? How can we adjust something to improve time? The following settings are available:

- **Parameters in zabbix_server.conf**: These are two in number. They offer a bit of control over the housekeeper. We have MaxHousekeeperDelete, which defines the maximum amount of records (from a table, field, or value) that will be removed in a housekeeper run. Larger numbers require more runtime. We also have HousekeepingFrequency, which sets the sleep time for the next execution of the housekeeper. Longer executions require more time.

- **Zabbix GUI parameters**: These are many and can be accessed by the administration menu after housekeeping. Here, the controls are very large and granular:

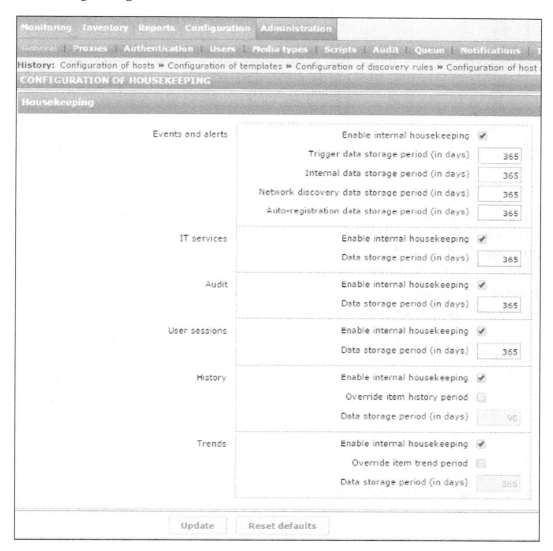

You shouldn't forget that some keys are specific to the Zabbix server and others to the Zabbix proxy.

For the Zabbix proxy, we have some interesting keys that should be used to help diagnose performance:

Internal key	Details
zabbix[process, "data sender",busy]	Here, we can see the maximum percentage of time for which the data sender was busy sending data to the Zabbix server. Higher numbers may indicate problems of network latency between the Zabbix proxy and Zabbix server.
zabbix[proxy_history]	This indicates the number of records in the Zabbix proxy's historical tables waiting to be sent to the Zabbix server. Higher numbers may indicate a lack of proxy pollers or trappers in the Zabbix server or some network problem.

It is also important to note that in the latest versions of Zabbix (at the time of writing this book, it is version 2.4), it is possible to manipulate the debug level for internal processes. This can be done using the runtime control parameter at the Zabbix server, Zabbix proxy, or Zabbix agent. The command is quite simple:

```
[root]# zabbix_server -R log_level_increase=poller,1
zabbix_server: command sent successfully
```

In this case, we increase the debug level only for the internal process poller number 1. Then, the log will contain more detailed information about this process.

Well, all of this is done so that you can see how necessary it is to know the depth of Zabbix. Hence, we can find the tuning and get the best performance out of our environment.

A suggestion is to visit the Zabbix manual, the internal checks part, and explore the possibilities of new items and triggers based on each existing key. The relevant part of the manual is at https://www.zabbix.com/documentation/2.4/manual/config/items/itemtypes/internal.

Database performance items

Database performance items are very important points and are overlooked by some users. We emphasize the importance of knowing the Zabbix server internally to get a correct reading of the data, and thereby make good corrective actions. We also need to know the Zabbix database parameters that can help us when making decisions and adjustments to the environment.

Each database has its peculiarity, and we must turn to the experts we have at home to support us with the data that we should collect and show us how we should evaluate that data.

As we have spoken of MySQL throughout this book, it is on this basis that we will address this topic. The trick is to use a MySQL collector that already has a ready metric and in which it is easy to incorporate new collections. Currently, DBforBIX is the most versatile gatherer that we can use to work with Zabbix. Its download and more information are available on the DBforBIX site at http://www.smartmarmot. com/product/dbforbix/.

The setup is simple; just follow the existing manual.

Which metrics should we get from the Zabbix database to support the performance settings? Some are quite relevant:

- **Slow queries**: Eventually, we will have a user demanding a lot from the Zabbix database. Knowing that the amount of slow queries will help us know that something different is happening in the environment.

- **Threads currently running**: These are the threads that are working and waiting for a function of the OS or hardware. A high number means some strain on the environment.

- **Quantity of DELETE, INSERT, SELECT, and UPDATE**: It is important to consider these four values together. It's normal to have a line-up with SELECT, DELETE, UPDATE, and INSERT.

Other metrics should also be evaluated, and it all depends on which database we use and what the Zabbix requirement is. If we have a better CPU, we have more memory and faster disks too.

In practice we need to know, as we have said, the application behavior so that we know exactly how to adjust the database settings. The following screenshot shows some data collected using Dbforbix and sent to Zabbix through SQL statements:

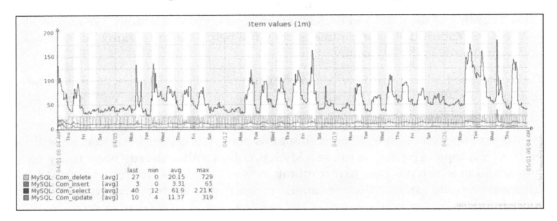

Summary

In this chapter, you learned that it is necessary to collect the monitoring environment data (Zabbix server proxy, database, and GUI) so that we know which performance tuning to do. You also learned that each component has its specific collections. For example, the Zabbix server has internal keys, and the Zabbix database can have your data collected by Dbforbix. We also need to pay attention to monitoring services, applications, and processes that are running to perform monitoring of the rest of the production environment.

In the next (and last) chapter, we will improve your understanding of the extent of monitoring, in addition to the infrastructure. We will try to show that Zabbix can (in my view, should) focus on the monitoring of the entire business and not just the infrastructure. That's the next challenge — meeting all levels of organizational structure:

- **Operating system**: This plays an important role because it is the basis of all components. It can generate bottlenecks that are often unknown.

- **Hardware**: This is as important as the operating system. It is the simplest to solve. If the hardware is exhausted, you just have to buy a new one. Often, the hardware is underutilized because the other components are misconfigured.

- **Storage**: This is directly related to the hardware, operating system, and database engine. It is where data is generated and handled by the application.

All of these components should always be considered when we are thinking of monitoring the health of an environment.

Don't forget that Zabbix doesn't work alone and although very relevant, this is not the only point to note about performance.

11
The Next Challenge

We've got here reading about the ways to ensure the performance of Zabbix in our environment. And since that has been achieved, what's next?

No doubt, the power of Zabbix is already something noticeable to whoever is reading this chapter. If performance has become a concern, it is because Zabbix is catering too much to the environment and there are a large number of users accessing the data collected in the environment.

But which approach are we using in Zabbix in our environment? Is it a tool to use in the technical area? Do some managers and coordinators also use Zabbix? What about the board of directors? Are all the organizational levels (operational, tactical, and strategic) using Zabbix?

The point is exactly how Zabbix can get more space in the environment. If you have solved the performance issues that could impact users' perception of Zabbix in a negative way, what's next?

We should keep our focus after key performance settings, on the following points:

- Identifying the sponsors of Zabbix
- Demands of business areas
- Developing dashboards
- Zabbix reports
- IT services or SLA reports

Identifying the sponsors of Zabbix

Once we have secured Zabbix's performance and users are satisfied with it, we can, in advance, think about the use of Zabbix in other areas of the company. After all, Zabbix has enough power to cater well beyond the IT environment.

Since a long time, we have addressed the issue of monitoring more broadly. Some institutes have studies and research showing a trend that companies are now trying to monitor the entire business and not just the infrastructure. This is not a new movement; we have already had significant moves towards it. The good news is that Zabbix fits well in this scenario and can act as a single console for monitoring that may be necessary in the environment, be it infrastructure monitoring or business monitoring.

Now our role is to identify the sponsors of Zabbix in our company. After that, we need to identify what services and business processes need to be monitored by these sponsors. At this point, what is worth our bargaining power, business vision, and political strength to leverage the use of Zabbix in the company?

Certainly, managers and directors need to see the business from the point of view of the systems and technologies that support existing processes. We've mentioned a few times in previous chapters that for many users, it makes sense that a trigger highlights a technical problem, such as a network asset being down or a database with full area.

The Zabbix sponsors in other areas of the company are users, who are not technicians, but will need information about the behavior of processes and services that satisfy the users of their area.

Be it an e-commerce site, a logistics company, hospital, bank, retail or any other business, there will be metrics that can be collected by Zabbix and are not technical. Our aim should be to meet our business's demands and identify the sponsors of each area. After this, we must know the metrics that are important to these users and then make Zabbix work to gather and evaluate these metrics.

The trick is to think of monitoring as a pyramid where the base is formed by monitoring related to physical and logical infrastructure (operational view). The middle portion is formed by the applications, transactions, routines, batch processes, and so on that are supported by the previous layer (tactical view). The top is formed by the final user service, general health of the environment, or other relevant metrics on that level (strategic vision).

The following diagram represents this view:

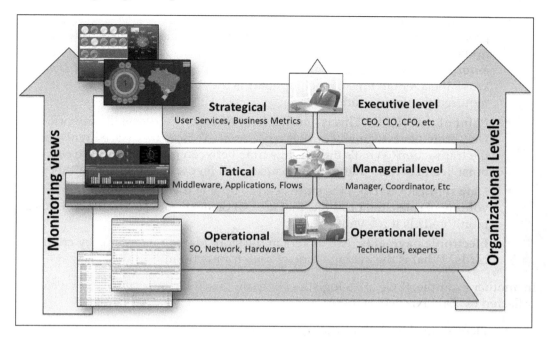

At each level, we have different user profiles with different requirements. At the bottom of the pyramid (operational view), Zabbix native screens and views are enough. For subsequent layers (tactical vision and strategic vision), we need something more customized, and this will often be achieved with some development using Zabbix API.

The fact is that it is not enough to have technical arguments to convince users who are not technical. We need to find valid arguments for each organizational level. The important thing is to understand that Zabbix can meet all of these requirements and we will not need other monitoring tools in our environment. This makes the operating environment much simpler because the technical teams won't need to know or receive training on various tools.

The demands in business areas

In this topic, we will illustrate some possible approaches with Zabbix in each area within our company.

For example, if we are a retail company, we have several things that can be monitored:

- **Product update process**: In any retail company, there is a need to update products, prices, stock, and so on. In other words, the stores need the lists of updated products, and this replication is certainly made by the company's **enterprise resource planning (ERP)**. But is this process monitored? Do we know the average time of each update? Is the throughput used? Or is it required for the upgrade?

- **Point of sale (POS)**: This is another item on any existing retail network. Does it matter how many outlets have opened? How many are involved in the transaction? What's the average time between transactions? We can, and must, lead users so that they indicate which metrics are relevant at this point.

- **Data replication**: Does the store need to update the matrix about the volume of sales, the products that are out of stock, and so on? Should this be monitored? Is it relevant?

- **Electronic payments**: Are buyers in the store making payments by credit cards? What is the average time of each transaction?

In another example, if we are a logistics company, we have other metrics that can be collected by Zabbix, such as these:

- **Fleet state**: Any logistics company has the fleet. How is the fleet going? How many trucks have stopped? Who's running it? Average speed?

- **Location**: Is the GPS on or off? Is there any route deviation?

In a hospital, these are what we can consider:

- **Reception**: Average waiting time for care, queue service by priority, and so on

- **Beds**: Patients calling for nurses, empty beds and occupied beds, and so on

In an e-commerce site, we should consider the following:

- **Store**: Online users, users making payments, users choosing products, withdrawals, the purchasing time, and user experience (Zabbix web monitoring)

- **Stock**: Low-stock products, the most sold product in the last hour, and so on

Of course, many of these metrics are already provided, or will be provided, by ERP or the existing management system, but this information can be cross-referenced with the availability of IT services. This makes it simpler to realize the impact of a service on a host whatsoever. The prioritization of the incident can be made based on its impact on the business.

The preceding list is only one example of the business metrics that can be collected and evaluated by Zabbix. Our role is to know our business to the point of provoking users of other areas to make them realize the importance of collecting and evaluating business data.

Each reader is definitely going to imagine what metrics are relevant and can be collected, either with a query in the applications database, or simulating user action with Zabbix web monitoring. The important thing is not to forget to engage users from other areas in search of new metrics.

Developing dashboards

Once these metrics have been identified and collected and the triggers have been created to evaluate the status of each business service, we need a presentation layer that is appropriate for the target audience.

From Zabbix version 1.8 onwards, we can make use of the Zabbix API to support us in this direction. We know that Zabbix has a powerful data collection engine that can access any data on any device. We also know that the Zabbix GUI has a large focus on the operational view of the environment. It works great for the technical user, but our challenge now is to take Zabbix to other areas of the company where the users are not technicians. It is very likely that at this point, the Zabbix GUI doesn't meet the requirements of these users.

Before setting out for a kind of development using the Zabbix API, we need to explore most of the Zabbix GUI. With graphics, maps, screens, and slide shows of Zabbix, we can create many interesting dashboards. Explore these resources to the maximum. It will, no doubt, be amazing to create new ways to view data by combining these features. The following are a few tips:

- **Graph**: Use different items to change the side of the axis. For example, we compare the use of the web server CPU with the volume of transactions by credit cards. These values will have different magnitudes, but we can see them in a single graph.

- **Maps**: Here, the possibilities are enormous. We import background and iconic images to mount a display layer that is very rich in detail. We may also use labels and macros to add metrics information to the map.

- **Screens**: This is another world full of possibilities. We know that all maps and graphics (among other things) can be combined in screens. Also, note that we can add external URLs to the cells of Zabbix screens. That is, you can put into Zabbix a URL of the application or system being monitored.

- **Slideshow**: This is another feature that helps Zabbix in the presentation layer. The screens, maps, and graphics can be combined into slides that alternate with each other and display a large amount of data.

With the native capabilities of Zabbix, we have managed to achieve much of what users need as a way to display data.

But what about the case when these features do not meet the expectations of users? Or when our director draws what he wants to see on a piece of paper? Or when he shows the dashboard of his dreams in a magazine? Can we manage to reproduce this with Zabbix? Certainly, yes! How? Using the Zabbix API. The trick is to study a little about the API and the programming languages that already have bindings for the Zabbix API.

On the Zabbix SIA website, we have a good source of information on possible starting points for the use of the Zabbix API at `http://www.zabbix.org/wiki/Docs/api/libraries`.

In addition to the Zabbix API, we can also list some toolkits to integrate with Zabbix and generate dashboards. Here are some starting points:

- `http://dashboarddude.com/`: This is a website created by an Australian who lives in Canada and provides tips and information about dashboards.
- `http://www.sencha.com/products/extjs`: A framework for development that can be integrated with Zabbix to create dashboards.
- `http://www.highcharts.com/`: A great alternative to integrate with Zabbix. It has an API that makes things a lot easier.
- `http://www.jqplot.com/`: Another JavaScript library that can be integrated with Zabbix.

I reiterate that the preceding list is not definitive, and other tools can be integrated with Zabbix and enable the creation of attractive dashboards for layers above the operational view. I have no doubt that graphics and dashboards generated with these tools will be more engrossing and help leverage Zabbix in your company.

Zabbix reports

Here is a very sensitive point for Zabbix's users: how can we extract Zabbix reports? In the Zabbix GUI, we have the report option in the main menu. Basically, the existing reports are as follows:

- **Availability report**: This is the most elaborate of all. It brings us information about the triggers and the time each trigger stayed in alert status. The view can be viewed by the trigger or host.

- **Triggers top 100**: This is quite important. It gives us information about the state changes of triggers, that is, we can get to know the repeat triggers.

- **Bar reports**: This seems to be a report forgotten by most users. We talk very little about it in forums, and in-training users don't show much interest either. However, the extracted information of this report may reveal a lot. For example, we can compare the average hourly CPU usage of the last 3 months from all hosts for a group.

These are Zabbix's native reports. Are they sufficient to meet the demands of our users? If not, how do we meet the demand? With the API! Again, this feature is an alternative to support the extraction and display of data.

Be sure to visit the suggested websites in the previous section; they are very useful at this point. In addition, we can think of the integration of Zabbix with specific tools for reporting or even **business intelligence (BI)**, such as these:

- **Pentaho** (http://www.pentaho.com/): It is a well-known BI. It has a powerful framework for reporting.

- **Jaspersoft** (http://www.jaspersoft.com/): This was well-known and popular for a long time. It remains a good alternative for integration with Zabbix.

- **Birt** (http://eclipse.org/birt/): It has IBM as one of its project sponsors, and has grown in recent years.

You are likely to come across other pieces of software that can be integrated with Zabbix. If some software supports JSON as the data source, then we have the best scenario for integration.

The trick is to know the expectations of the sponsored users of Zabbix in other areas, and try to meet this expectation in some way. For this, we often need to integrate Zabbix with other platforms.

IT services or SLA reports

Another way to meet the business areas of our company is to create an SLA tree so that services can be monitored by considering the link with the other monitored layers (operational and tactical).

Usually, an isolated trigger doesn't serve to represent the service and all of its environmental dependencies. It is something like this: a service to the user depends on certain infrastructure components, and these dependencies need to be represented in the SLA reports. Its format is like a tree, where we have the root, trunk, branches, and leaves, and they will be represented by triggers.

SLA reports in Zabbix are — in some environments — in the background, and Zabbix administrators end up not using this resource. But it is important to bear in mind that this feature is one that helps us leverage Zabbix within our company, because it can establish a not-so-technical vision and is more focused on the business.

The important thing is to try to make up at SLA report, not the infrastructure, but the relationship of the user with the service infrastructure. An appropriate structure of SLA tree would look like this:

Concept	Real-life example

• Root
  ○ Trunk A
    ▪ Branch AA
      • Leaf AAA
      • Leaf AAB
      • Leaf AAC
    ▪ Branch AB
      • Leaf ABA
      • Leaf ABB
      • Leaf ABC
  ○ Trunk B
    ▪ Branch BA
      • Leaf BAA
      • Leaf BAB
  ○ Trunk C
	• E-commerce
	  ○ Web server cluster
	    ▪ Apache01
	      • Users online
	      • Apache online
	      • Error log
	    ▪ Apache02
	      • Users online
	      • Apache online
	      • Error log
	  ○ Database
	    ▪ MySQL
	      • Online
	      • Max clients
	  ○ Network
	  ○ Energy

This approach will give us a consolidated and detailed view of the state of services that are operating in the environment.

This functionality is one of the most important for supporting Zabbix in our company. With SLA reports, we can confront facts and data with the perception of internal or external users. It is also of great value for IT teams when you highlight the availability of services for users.

To learn more about creating your tree services in Zabbix, visit the main page of this topic at `https://www.zabbix.com/documentation/2.4/manual/it_services`.

Summary

The challenge is to understand where and how Zabbix can support the company's business. Do not think of this powerful tool only as something to be used to monitor the IT infrastructure.

Identifying potential internal Zabbix sponsors is essential to take the tool further and further. These users can have requirements that we can't perceive, and therefore fall outside our actions. Stay tuned, talk to people in other areas, and understand how Zabbix can help.

The creation of all of this—new monitoring, integrations, reporting, and dashboards—can have a great impact on the behavior and use of Zabbix and its components. So, we need to plan the growth of the environment.

Therefore, it is very important to go ahead with this approach only after ensuring that Zabbix is fully functional and is performing well. The challenge is precisely this: prepare Zabbix so that it supports not only the demands of IT but also the demands of other business areas. It is of no use trying to take Zabbix to other areas if it does not have adequate performance to meet the IT demands.

Throughout this book, we said that each environment will require its specific settings and adjustments, and there is no "configuration killer file" that works for all environments. This means that knowing your environment, the hardware at hand, Zabbix's behavior, the database engine that will be used, and user behavior is the key to successful implementation of Zabbix.

It is expected that all the information we covered throughout this book will help you understand environmental behavior and support you in planning the necessary adjustments.

At the time of writing this book, Zabbix is at version 2.4, and users have great expectations from Zabbix 3.0, which promises major changes in internal concepts and approaches. No doubt, improvement in performance is one of the topics that Zabbix SIA will not leave out in this new version.

Whoever made it this far is certainly determined to use or maintain Zabbix on their environment. I have no doubt that this is the best decision. The decision that I took in 2006 was to migrate all our monitoring platforms (six in total) to Zabbix. With each new release, we have strengthened this conviction, with the improvements made by Zabbix SIA.

I hope that reading this book has been pleasant and has created a need to reassess the existing concepts so far. This is because reviewing concepts and making decisions is the best way to evolve.

Index

A

accelerators
  Alternative PHP cache (APC) 55
  eAccelerator 55
  XCache 55
active items 27, 28
Alternative PHP cache (APC)
  URL 55
Apache
  compression 52
Apache Bench (AB) tool 56

B

Birt
  URL 121
BufferSend parameter 28
BufferSize parameter 28
business intelligence (BI) 121
business monitoring 11

C

caches and buffers
  about 32, 34
  CacheSize (configuration cache) 32
  HistoryCacheSize (history cache) 33
  HistoryTextCacheSize (history text
    cache 33
  TrendCacheSize (trends cache) 33
  ValueCache (value cache) 33
complaints 49, 50
components
  dividing 80
  for hardware, specifying 81-85

compression
  in Apache 52
  in lighttpd 53
  in Nginx 54
  testing 54

D

dashboards
  developing 119
databases
  comparing 39-43
  main configuration parameters 44
  performance items 111references, URL 44
DBSyncers 35, 36
default templates 34

E

eAccelerator
  URL 55
enterprise resource planning (ERP) 118
environment
  classifying 65, 66

F

firewall settings 95

H

hardware, for Zabbix proxy 96
HP
  URL 74

I

innodb_buffer_pool_instances
parameter 45
innodb_buffer_pool_size parameter 45
innodb_flush_log_at_trx_commit
parameter 45
innodb_flush_method parameter 46
innodb_io_capacity parameter 46
innodb_log_file_size parameter 46
Intelligent Platform Management Interface
(IPMI) 13
International Telecommunication Union
(ITU) 17
Internet of Things (IoT) 16-19
I/O scheduler values
anticipatory 74
completely fair queuing (CFQ) 73
deadline 73
NOOP 74
item types
about 24-26
and performance 24-26
simple check 25
SNMP trap 25
Zabbix agent 24
Zabbix agent (active) 25
Zabbix aggregate 25
Zabbix trapper 25

J

Jaspersoft
URL 121
Java Management Extensions (JMX) 13

K

kernel
adjustment 70
kernel-level FD limits 71-77
user-level FD limits 71
kernel-level FD limits
about 71, 72
vm.dirty_background_ratio parameter 73
vm.dirty_ratio parameter 73

L

lighttpd
compression 53
Linux distributions
Zabbix 69, 70
local storage
and shared storage, selecting
between 59-63

M

main configuration parameters
about 44, 52
compression, in Apache 52
compression, in lighttpd 53
compression, in Nginx 54
innodb_buffer_pool_instances 45
innodb_buffer_pool_size 45
innodb_flush_log_at_trx_commit 45
innodb_flush_method 46
innodb_io_capacity 46
innodb_log_file_size 46
tmpdir 46
metrics, Zabbix database
slow queries 111
threads currently running 111
values 111

N

natural growth
controlling 13-15
new values per second (nvps) 6
Nginx
compression 54

O

Open Database Connectivity (ODBC) 13
Oracle
URL 74

P

Pentaho
URL 121

PHP accelerator
  advantages 55
point of sale (POS) 118
primer monitoring 61
proxy internal items
  and server 102-108
  metrics 103-105
  Zabbix GUI parameters 109
  zabbix_server.conf, parameters 108

S

shared storage
  and local storage, selecting between 59-63
Simple Network Management Protocol
    (SNMP) 13
SLA reports 122
small and medium enterprises (SME) 12
sponsors, Zabbix
  identifying 116
storage for performance
  configuring 63-65
system monitoring 11

T

tables
  partitioning 85-88
tmpdir parameter 46
trigger functions
  about 28
  avg() function 29
  last() function 29
  max() function 29
  min() function 29
  nodata() function 29
tuning
  for reading 47
  for writing 47

V

values per second (VPS) 49

W

web servers
  differences 50, 51
  URL 51

X

XCache
  URL 55

Z

Zabbix
  about 4, 19, 115
  and SQL fields 26, 27
  API, URL 120
  best practices 4
  beyond infrastructure 16
  business areas, demands 117-119
  CacheSize parameter 82
  challenges 6, 7
  complaints 49
  components, dividing 79, 80
  components, virtualizing 60
  dashboards, developing 119, 120
  database 6
  data types 26
  don'ts 8
  environment, prerequisites 66, 67
  error 3
  evolution 2
  GUI 5
  hardware for component, specifying 81
  HistoryCacheSize parameter 82
  history tables 30
  HistoryTextCacheSize parameter 83
  improvements 20
  initial steps 12, 13
  IT services 121, 123
  Linux distributions 70
  manual, URL 30, 110
  performance 20, 90-92
  performance, URL 20
  proxy 6, 90-92
  queue 100
  reference links 20
  reports 120
  right tool, selecting 2, 3
  server 5
  simplifying 5, 6
  SLA reports 122, 123
  sponsors, identifying 116, 117
  tree services, URL 123

TrendCacheSize parameter 83
trend tables 30, 31
URL 39
ValueCacheSize parameter 83
VMwareCacheSize parameter 82
website references, URL 120
working with 9, 10
Zabbix 1.0
about 24
license, URL 24
Zabbix, don'ts
default database settings, using 8
default templates, using 8
lack of planning 8
Zabbix GUI
graph 119
maps 119
screens 119
slideshow 120
Zabbix proxy
about 89-92
ConfigFrequency parameter 93
DataSenderFequency parameter 94
hardware 96

HeartbeatFrequency parameter 93
Hostname parameter 93
internal keys 110
ProxyConfigFrequency parameter 94
ProxyDataFrequency parameter 95
ProxyLocalBuffer parameter 93
ProxyMode parameter 93
ProxyOfflineBuffer parameter 93
ProxyPollers parameter 94
Server parameter 94
ServerPort parameter 94
steps 92
Zabbix queue
about 100-102
delay 102
LastClock 102
Zabbix reports
availability report 121
bar reports 121
extracting 120

Thank you for buying
Zabbix Performance Tuning

About Packt Publishing

Packt, pronounced 'packed', published its first book, *Mastering phpMyAdmin for Effective MySQL Management*, in April 2004, and subsequently continued to specialize in publishing highly focused books on specific technologies and solutions.

Our books and publications share the experiences of your fellow IT professionals in adapting and customizing today's systems, applications, and frameworks. Our solution-based books give you the knowledge and power to customize the software and technologies you're using to get the job done. Packt books are more specific and less general than the IT books you have seen in the past. Our unique business model allows us to bring you more focused information, giving you more of what you need to know, and less of what you don't.

Packt is a modern yet unique publishing company that focuses on producing quality, cutting-edge books for communities of developers, administrators, and newbies alike. For more information, please visit our website at www.packtpub.com.

About Packt Open Source

In 2010, Packt launched two new brands, Packt Open Source and Packt Enterprise, in order to continue its focus on specialization. This book is part of the Packt Open Source brand, home to books published on software built around open source licenses, and offering information to anybody from advanced developers to budding web designers. The Open Source brand also runs Packt's Open Source Royalty Scheme, by which Packt gives a royalty to each open source project about whose software a book is sold.

Writing for Packt

We welcome all inquiries from people who are interested in authoring. Book proposals should be sent to author@packtpub.com. If your book idea is still at an early stage and you would like to discuss it first before writing a formal book proposal, then please contact us; one of our commissioning editors will get in touch with you.

We're not just looking for published authors; if you have strong technical skills but no writing experience, our experienced editors can help you develop a writing career, or simply get some additional reward for your expertise.

Zabbix Cookbook

ISBN: 978-1-78439-758-6   Paperback: 260 pages

Over 70 hands-on recipes to get your infrastructure up and running with Zabbix

1. Set up and configure your own Zabbix server by using packages or from source.

2. Automate your Zabbix infrastructure in order to maintain your Zabbix setup.

3. Create your own items and use them to monitor your Zabbix infrastructure with the help of this practical, step-by-step guide.

Zabbix Network Monitoring Essentials

ISBN: 978-1-78439-976-4   Paperback: 178 pages

Your one-stop solution to efficient network monitoring with Zabbix

1. Effectively monitor a number of network devices based on network security and segments.

2. Adapt your monitoring solution to an array of evolving network scenarios using Zabbix discovery features.

3. A fast-paced guide to Zabbix network monitoring with a strategic focus on the collection and organization of data.

PACKT PUBLISHING

open source
community experience distilled

Mastering Zabbix

ISBN: 978-1-78328-349-1   Paperback: 358 pages

Monitor your large IT environment efficiently with Zabbix

1. Create the perfect monitoring configuration based on your specific needs.

2. Extract reports and visualizations from your data.

3. Integrate monitoring data with other systems in your environment.

4. Learn the advanced techniques of Zabbix to monitor networks and performances in large environments.

Zabbix Network Monitoring Essentials [Video]

ISBN: 978-1-78216-550-7   Duration: 02:33 hours

Leverage the advanced features of Zabbix to set up a professional network monitoring system quickly and efficiently

1. Get a fast-paced tour through the essential parts of Zabbix.

2. Set up your own monitoring system so Zabbix can inform you if your IT infrastructure starts misbehaving.

3. Learn to make practical use of features you won't find in the documentation.

Please check **www.PacktPub.com** for information on our titles

www.ingramcontent.com/pod-product-compliance
Lightning Source LLC
Chambersburg PA
CBHW082120070326
40690CB00049B/4006